ARCHITECTURE BY
BIRDS AND INSECTS

WRITTEN AND ILLUSTRATED BY Peggy Macnamara

CONTRIBUTORS
John M. Bates and James H. Boone

WITH A FOREWORD BY
David Quammen

ARCHITECTURE BY

BIRDS AND INSECTS

A NATURAL ART

THE UNIVERSITY OF CHICAGO PRESS

IN ASSOCIATION WITH THE FIELD MUSEUM

CHICAGO AND LONDON

PEGGY MACNAMARA is associate professor at
the School of the Art Institute in Chicago, artist-in-
residence and associate of the Zoology Department at
The Field Museum, and author of *Painting Wildlife in
Watercolor* and *Illinois Insects and Spiders*. She exhibits
at Packer Schopf Gallery in Chicago, and her work can
be seen on exhibit throughout The Field Museum.

The University of Chicago Press, Chicago 60637
The University of Chicago Press, Ltd., London
© 2008 by The University of Chicago
All rights reserved. Published 2008
Printed in China

17 16 15 14 13 12 11 10 09 08   1 2 3 4 5

ISBN-13: 978-0-226-50097-3 (cloth)
ISBN-10: 0-226-50097-7 (cloth)

Published in association with The Field Museum

The poem "Nests" by Robert Cording was originally
published in *Against Consolation* (CavanKerry Press,
2002).

The paper used in this publication meets the minimum
requirements of the American National Standard for In-
formation Sciences—Permanence of Paper for Printed
Library Materials, ANSI Z39.48–1992.

Library of Congress Cataloging-in-Publication Data
Macnamara, Peggy.
Architecture by birds and insects : a natural art /
written and illustrated by Peggy Macnamara ;
contributors, John M. Bates and James H. Boone ;
with a foreword by David Quammen.
    p. cm.
ISBN-13: 978-0-226-50097-3 (cloth : alk. paper)
ISBN-10: 0-226-50097-7 (cloth : alk. paper)
1. Birds—Nests.
2. Birds—Nests—Pictorial works.
3. Insects—Habitations.
4. Insects—Habitations—Pictorial works.
I. Bates, John M., 1951—   II. Boone, James H.
III. Title.
QL675.M33 2008
598.156′4—dc22
                                20077031847

FOR JACK MACNAMARA,

who built and sustained the nest for the past thirty-six years

CONTENTS

FOREWORD

by David Quammen

Nesting is a very old form of animal behavior, dating back at least tens of millions of years. Birds do it, bees do it, termites do it, alligators do it—and paleontology tells us that even dinosaurs did it. I heard that point forcefully made about twenty years ago, by a paleontologist named Jack Horner, as we sat on a bare hillside in north central Montana, near the spot where he had found a nest of fifteen baby dinosaurs. Well . . . what he had found, more precisely, was a passel of fossilized baby-dinosaur bones, which when he sorted them out yielded fifteen individuals and several intriguing clues. Clue one: the fifteen babies had lived for a short time after hatching—as testified by marks of wear on their teeth—and then had died of some indeterminable cause. Clue two: at death, they were still cowering together within an artificially made depression, a scooped-out place, rather than scattered randomly roundabout. A mudslide had covered them; they were converted chemically from bone into stone; and there they lay for about seventy million years, until Jack and his crew of skilled diggers happened along.

What was notable about these dinosaur infants, Jack explained, was that they had *stayed in their nest* after hatching and been fed there, presumably by their mother. The little fossils, and the clues embodied in them, revealed a striking new fact about saurian behavior: that at least some dinosaur species were capable of supplying parental care. That is, of mothering (maybe fathering also, but that's a more tenuous bet) in the extended sense. They didn't just bury their eggs and depart, like a sea turtle. They didn't spawn and die, like a salmon. They came and went, to and from the site of delivery, bringing food like a robin, tending their young. The proof—tender juveniles, huddled together, with worn teeth—was in the nest.

Take any other nest, of any other species, and you can work backward to a similar story. Nest building and other forms of architecture (colony building among ants or termites, den building among beavers or bears, bed building among chimpanzees or gorillas) are a forceful and pragmatic instinct seen in all sorts of animals. We humans tend to think in strict categories, separating *nature* and *art* as one of our definitive dichotomies, but between those two stands *artifice* as practiced by many of our nonhuman fellows. And every nest represents a story, a piece of evidence, from which ecological deductions can be drawn. Take a bird, take an insect; look at its nest—look *carefully*—and you can begin to ask: What challenges did this creature face in the struggle to win a mate and reproduce? What sort of threats, what sort of elements, what sort of enemies did its offspring confront? How did it provide against those threats? In what forms have the raw imperatives of sex and survival come to express themselves as protective architecture?

That's the subject addressed by Peggy Macnamara and her contributors in this graceful, richly illustrated book. But more than that, it is keenly informative and ecologically astute, as well as lovely. Macnamara and her colleagues demonstrate an important truth: you can know a lot about a person, or a critter, from where he or she lives.

NESTS

by Robert Cording

More than we imagined,
visible now that we can see
through the leafless branches—

nests, in the lilacs, near
the trunk of a weeping cherry,
on a maple branch horizon.

In them, the past
summer: dead grasses,
milkweed and dandelion

down, our lost cat's
white fur, line I cut
from a fishing reel, bits

of scattered fingernail-
sized eggshells—a robin's
pale blue and, the color

of century-old photographs,
with spots of two shades
of brown on cream, the remains

of a phoebe's eggs. Over
seven days in June 1855,
Thoreau filled a journal

with quick jottings on tens
of nests—date, place,
type—as he tried to teach

his eyes to *saunter*, to celebrate
without ordering what was
gathered from odds and ends

and sown here and there
like the random matter of creation.
We try, too, but find ourselves

looking at these nests as if they
Were old letters or diaries
that conceal as much as they

confide about a world
scattered with bits of narrative,
a story we cannot quite tell

and cannot keep from telling.

INTRODUCTION
by Peggy Macnamara

There are many other things more godlike in their nature than man . . . for whatever provides all things well for itself, to this (one) would apply the term practically wise.

ARISTOTLE, NICOMACHEAN ETHICS

Holding in my hand a tiny wasp nest with a roof, I felt like I had come home. Nests are little works of art, built with care and precision, confident and complete. They work! Dressed in comfortable colors, the whole range of earth tones, they reflect my palette. Best of all they are of use, providing a service. They are natural materials recycled to create homes and safe places to nurture and protect young, while also integrating into the surrounding environment. I have always preferred art with a purpose: Chinese pots, medieval manuscripts, gothic churches, and even contemporary installations whose purpose seems to be to make us laugh at our-

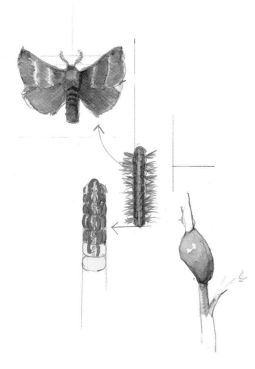

selves (e.g., Charles Ray's *Family Romance*). The best art doesn't "show off." It is the simplest of solutions, working on many levels.

The nests illustrated here are, with a couple of exceptions, drawn from the collections of the Field Museum, my home for the past twenty-five years. Each nest brings with it a story of instinct being honed and improved, the same process used by artists to build on history and solve universal problems.

I can't help but be amazed by these constructions, and I marvel at the animals' instinct. I don't intend to add to the scientific debate on the subject, but merely to reflect on my own experience of tapping into instincts when making art. I believe it is the secret that takes art beyond a technical human endeavor. It comes down to personal choices, made not intellectually but instinctively. It is this parallel with the instinct of animals that most fascinates me. They work as I do: slowly, persistently, and calling on the invisible answers of instinct.

While drawing in the public exhibit spaces of the Field Museum as artist-in-residence, I am often asked, "Why collect?" Collecting is about gaining knowledge and sharing that knowledge to better understand our world. Finding Robert Gregg's extensive collection of insect nests on a subfloor of the Field Museum was like discovering a silent treasure. His lifetime of collecting around the world was tucked away in several cabinets, each specimen wrapped, labeled, and placed in an old box.

Robert E. Gregg of Boulder, Colorado, retired professor of biology at the University of Colorado in Boulder, donated his large collection of ants and other insects to the Field Museum of Natural History, Department of Zoology, and Division of Insects in 1992. His collection included 600,000 specimens of ants, representing about a thousand species worldwide. This collection includes over a hundred nests and voucher specimens for Gregg's book, *Ants of Colorado*, a classic systematic and ecological study.

Sometimes the insect responsible was placed in a jar alongside the nest. Other times I would pick up the nest and its designer would just fall out. The Field Museum's vast collections include both insect and bird nests. In addition to Gregg's, many of the insect nests are part of the Dr. B. E. Dahlgren donation collected by Samuel Harris in 1923 and 1925 from Demerara, British Guiana (now Guyana). The donation included three thousand specimens and 160 wasp and ant nests. Bird nests were likewise gathered on expeditions all over the world. This book would not exist without collections.

After working on specimens in the off-exhibit areas of the museum, I ventured back into the public exhibit "Animal Kingdom." I thought I had seen everything on public display, but I had missed most of the nests. Their abstract nature made them look like installations possibly found in a contemporary art gallery. At the same time their unobtrusiveness and natural colors made them almost invisible in the cases and dioramas. I began seeing in a new light some of the museum's old dioramas, such as the one featuring the bowerbird. Although the particular structure of interest here is not a nest, this exhibit shows the efforts of a plain-looking bird so intent on luring a mate that he built a bower of grasses and decorated it with hundreds of stones, shells, and bones. The Field Museum dioramas and collected specimens and the nests I myself found in Evanston provided the diverse sources for my watercolors.

I previously thought that bird nests were uniform and primarily cup-shaped until I saw cliff swallows building their caves near the lake and geese removing packing materials, paper, straw, and cotton from a local building site and recycling them into a nest. I found that birds also sewed, worked in clay, manufactured substances, and regulated their nest temperature. Once these avid builders caught my attention, I was hooked. Winter cleared their "cover" and left bird and insect nests exposed. It was like a coming-out party. In January, I couldn't wait to take down old hornet nests to study their "insides." Spring brought the possibilities of finding treasures with every walk. After storms you can find abandoned nests, fallen from trees. I have a site I check at my corner every morning, just hoping. . . . Spring also brings back the red-winged blackbirds who shoo me away from their hidden nest sites in lakeshore shrubs. They think my brown hair is the work of a fellow nester and swoop and peck at my head, defending their territory and signaling that they will have none of that in their neighborhood.

After painting for a couple of years, I saw my images begin to take shape as one story about the miraculous parallels within the animal kingdom. Moreover, I found that humans were still using the techniques and materials common to both birds and insects. These life-size versions of nests could be found in the adobes of South America, the conical stone domes in Turkey, and the thatched circular huts from Venezuela. The small floating islands in Inle Lake, Myanmar, which are sold and traded, resemble larger versions of a grebe's nest. From this point on it was easy to find architects speaking to the same issues and solutions as insects and birds.

The architect most akin to nature's builders is Samuel Mockbee, creator of the Rural Studio and a professor at Auburn University. Using salvaged lumber, old tires, concrete rubble, and other discarded materials, he and his students constructed inexpensive buildings in a style he described as "contemporary modernism grounded in Southern culture." In a world where there is too much waste and not enough housing, Mockbee's elegant solutions garnered him a MacArthur "genius" grant. But the truth is insects and birds have been doing this forever.

For the artist in all of us, what is to be learned from birds and insects and their architectural feats? It is the value of listening to our instincts, recycling our natural resources, and using our accumulated experience to solve problems.

According to Aristotle, "Science is the union of knowledge and intuition and has for its subjects those things which are most precious in their nature." Nests are objects of art and also pure science, because each carries with it a complex and precious story of how and why. These tales also illuminate our own experiences and make us wonder and want to understand more about the work of the smaller creatures around us.

PLATES

The Montezuma Oropendola

The Montezuma Oropendola (*Psarcolius montezuma*), a large member of the oriole family (Icteridae) native to Central America, is a dark brown bird with bright yellow tail feathers. Oropendola roughly means "gold pendulum"; the pendulum part is descriptive of the bird's nest, a long, narrow woven basket, from 1 to 2 meters (about 3.2 to 6.5 feet) long. Each nest holds one adult female and her offspring. Nests hang from the highest branches of tall trees, sometimes by the dozens or even hundreds.

The Oropendola species have interesting symbiotic relationships with cowbirds and wasps. Accounts vary, but in one, Oropendolas like to nest in trees where hornets are found because the hornets keep away the parasitic cowbirds; the Oropendolas, in turn, protect the hornets from bees. On the other hand, some say cowbirds are desirable nest parasites because they attack botflies, the real enemy. Botflies like to lay their eggs directly on the newly hatched Oropendolas, and the botfly larvae feed on the young birds. But cowbird eggs hatch before the Oropendola eggs do. Young cowbirds feed on the botflies, thus protecting the Oropendolas.

(For the caddisfly, see the text for plate III.)

1"

PLATE I

Variety of Bird Nests

The sumptuous variety of bird nests comes to life with this plate: clay pots and purse shapes, some tiny, some large; one glued together with saliva and many with spider webs. These nests are but a few examples of bird ingenuity that I found among the hundreds of nests in the Bird Division, on a sub-floor in the Field Museum. The hardest part in painting them was being forced to choose among them.

1 Common grackle

Order Passeriformes, family Icteridae, *Quiscalus quiscula*

It takes the female common grackle eleven days to build her nest of weed stalks and grasses evenly arranged. The outside nest diameter is from seven to nine inches. The birds nest in colonies of twenty to thirty pairs up to sixty feet above ground.

2 Island scrub jay or Santa Cruz jay

Order Passeriformes, family Corvidae, *Aphelocoma insularis*

The Santa Cruz jay is one of a number of North American jay species. Its nest, about one foot in diameter, has a bulky and sturdy exterior of sticks and twigs and a soft interior of grasses and rootlets.

3 Eastern wood peewee

Order Passeriformes, family Tyrannidae, *Contopus virens*

Resting on a horizontal branch, the tiny eastern wood peewee nest is well hidden. The female constructs it with thick walls of grasses and stems and wraps it in spider webs. It is barely three inches in diameter.

4, 5 Northern (Baltimore) oriole, and chimney swift

Icterus galbula and *Chaetura pelagica*

(See plate XXXVI.)

6 African penduline tit

Order Passeriformes, family Remizidae, *Anthroscopus caroli*

The tiny African penduline tit constructs a nest about three inches long, with an opening at the top. It hangs like a bag and is composed of moss, fine bark, hair, and cobwebs.

7 Apostlebird

Order Passeriformes, family Corcoracidae, *Struthidea cinerea*

An apostlebird molded this clay pot nest by turning itself around and around. The feat was accomplished during breeding season at the Brookfield Zoo in Chicago, Illinois. The apostlebird is an Australian songbird in the family Corcoracidae, which includes the mudlark and white-winged chough. These three species are sometimes called "mud-nest builders." The nest has an outside diameter of seven inches.

Oecophylla smaragdina

PART ONE

Nests Made by Sewing, Weaving, and Binding

Ludwig Mies van der Rohe asked, while showing his audience a leaf hut and other primitive structures of walrus ribs and seal hides, "Have you ever seen anything more complete in fulfilling its function and in its use of materials? What feeling for material and what a power of expression speaks in these buildings. What warmth they radiate and how beautiful they are. They echo like old songs. . . ."

FROM *Mies van der Rohe: Architect as Educator*

Some species of both birds and insects bind and weave to create their shelters.

Weaving is the process of moving threads over and under other threads to form or build up fabric. Birds make good weavers because they use their beaks to push the thread through the fabric; they have well-coordinated head movements and good vision to follow the passage of the thread. The threads found in nature—grasses, plant fibers, and silk from spider webs and some caterpillar nests—are relatively short, only two or three times the length of the bird. So some birds make lots of knots to hold the fabric together. Sewing is used in nest building to attach pieces of material, such as two leaves. When the tailorbird sews, it passes stitches made out of spider silk and plant fibers through the leaves. The tailorbird, a small songbird, uses its beak and legs to perform these tasks.

Binding is achieved by combining blocks with an adhesive. Invertebrates commonly use silk for this purpose. The larvae of caddisflies and bagworms build houses around themselves by sticking materials together with silk. "Silk" is a generic term used to describe the thread produced by arthropods. The most common silk is the one produced by orb-weaving spiders and silkworms.

Sticks piled on top of each other become a compressed structural material that bears a load the same way a concrete block supports your weight when you stand on it. Nests built this way are strong because they are wider than they are tall, and the sticks create friction, which creates resistance in movement. These kinds of nests are built by larger birds, such as eagles and ospreys.

PLATE II

Sewing and Weaving

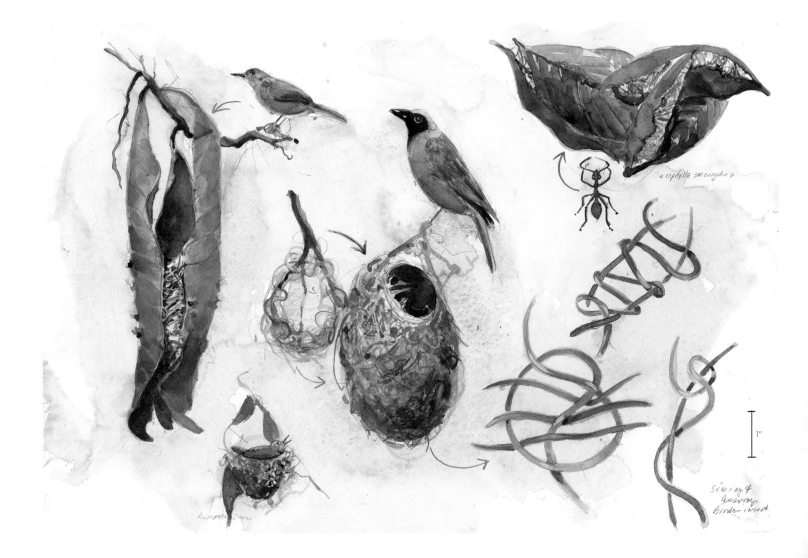

Oecophylla smaragdina

1"

Sewing &
Weaving
Birds–insect

humming birds

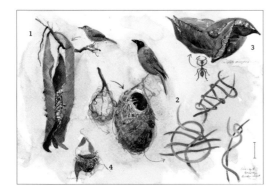

1 Dark-necked tailorbird

Order Passeriformes, family Sylviidae, *Orthotomus atrogularis*

Like a tailor sewing sides of fabric together with a needle, the dark-necked tailorbird (usually the female) of Asia sews together the sides of leaves to make her nest. She incorporates into her nest living leaves she finds on trees, providing a snug, waterproof home that is also well camouflaged. The bird curls the leaf by twisting spider web strands around it. She then makes tiny holes in the edges with her pointed bill, and through the holes she laces fibers from bark, cottony seed fibers, or spider webs. The opposites ends of these fibers are teased into balls, not knotted together. In the resulting pouch, the bird places grass lined with kapok and other soft, fluffy seeds.

2 Speke's weaver

Order Passeriformes, family Ploceidae, *Ploceus spekei*

Weavers or weaver birds comprise a large family from the Old World tropics. Members of the genus Ploceus are the true weavers, building intricately constructed nests. Speke's weavers live in the African highlands and nest away from water. The knots and loops of a weaver bird can be seen in the three examples on the bottom right. The bird works as both a basket weaver and a weaver with a loom. The male works for a week, weaving a loose nest, then tries to find a mate. If he doesn't succeed, he will dismantle his work and begin again, trying to build a better nest in the same spot. Weaver birds often nest in colonies (see page 22).

3 Weaver ant

Order Hymenoptera, family Formicidae,
Oecophylla smaragdina

Working in much the same way
as the tailorbird, these ants from
tropical areas of Africa and Australia
create a nest that is more like a ball
of leaves. Some workers hold the
edges of leaves together. Others hold
in their jaws live larvae that produce
the silk that binds the leaves together.
When this ball of leaves is disturbed,
the ants will repair the nest. They
hold on to the loose part of the leaf
with their legs, grab the other leaf
with their mandibles, and slowly
pull the two leaves closer by stepping
back.

4 Ruby-throated hummingbird

Order Apodiformes, family Trochilidae,
Archilochus colubris

Befitting her own tiny dimensions,
the ruby-throated hummingbird
of eastern North America builds a
nest no larger than a walnut, about 4
centimeters wide and 6 centimeters
tall (about 1.5 to 2.3 inches). She posi-
tions it on a sloping limb, often sheltered by other branches, overhanging
an open area or stream. Using silk
from spider webs or caterpillar nests
to bind it together, she makes the
nest of leaves and scales and cam-
ouflages it with lichens. Dandelion,
cattail, or thistle down softens the
inside for the laying of two white
eggs, 8 by 13 millimeters in size. The
nest will stretch to accommodate the
growing nestlings, which the mother
feeds on her own. She may revisit
and rebuild the nest for the following
year's brood.

ARTIST'S NOTE: *The order in their little constructions is amazing, and the results are like works of recycled art. Marcel Duchamp, who first exhibited already-made or found objects, could have learned something from the caddisfly. There are no labels on the next two plates because the specimens I chose were not identified to species.*

PLATE III

Caddisfly Larvae ORDER TRICHOPTERA

Closely related to moths and butterflies, caddisfly larvae look like caterpillars. They are aquatic as immatures, living in freshwater streams and lakes, becoming winged adults upon emerging. After the larvae hatch they begin to build small tubes around themselves, which will serve as their temporary homes while they mature to adults. They first surround themselves with silk from their salivary glands. They keep their abdomens safe inside the tubes and use their legs and mouth parts to gather material, cut it, and attach it to their casings. If they live in a moving stream, they will need materials from their environment heavy enough to weigh down their homes, like stones or shells, whereas if they live in stagnant water, lighter materials are more suitable. As the larvae grow they continually strengthen and enlarge these tubes with vegetation, sand, shells, or snails. Different species create different designs with different materials. These tiny architectural masterpieces provide perfect camouflage.

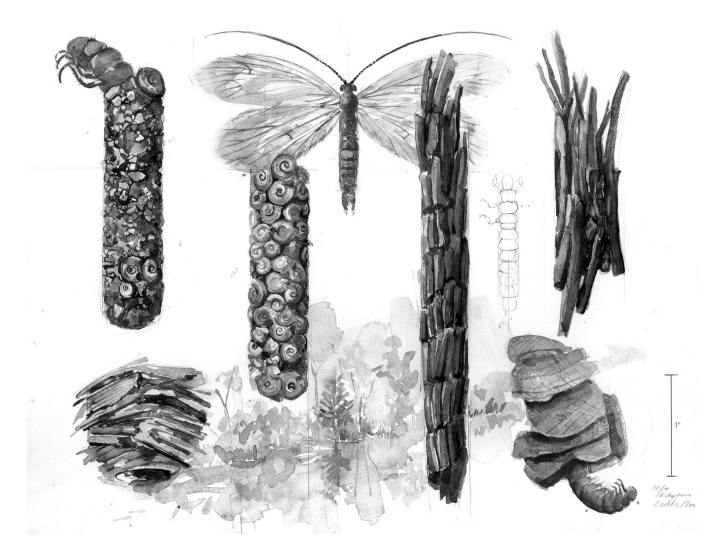

Order
Trichoptera
Caddis Flies

1"

ARTIST'S NOTE: *When I was first shown the cases of bagworm larvae, I could hardly believe my eyes: tiny, tidy examples of efficiency houses. Wrapped like mummies or shaped like sleeping bags, each specimen was of different materials, depending on what was available. The bagworm is a miniature reflection of the environmental sculpture of Christo and Jeanne-Claude. To understand them better, I made paintings of many of these specimens as large as five feet tall so I could experience them on a human scale.*

PLATE IV

Bagworm Larvae   ORDER LEPIDOPTERA, FAMILY PSYCHIDAE

Bagworms are moths, one to three inches long, that make cases similar to caddisflies, spinning little silken tubes to which they attach plant or soil particles. Like caddisflies, they arrange the building materials in longitudinal, transverse, or spiral patterns. This plate shows a variety of sizes and shapes of bagworm cases. The case materials serve as camouflage, making them hard for predators to see. They differ from the larvae of caddisflies in that they live on land and attach themselves to trees, where they feed on lichen, trees, and shrubs. Their little homes are both mobile and expandable—they enlarge as the larvae grow. The female adults in some species have no wings and remain in their bags. They release a chemical called "pheromone" that enables the males to find them. Eggs are laid inside the case in the fall, and the larvae hatch in the spring and start constructing their own cases.

1"

ARTIST'S NOTE: *A model of a life-size ant garden is on display at the Field Museum on the second floor outside the plant exhibit. I painted this plate from this diorama, which provided a new composition from every angle. The complexity of the diorama is like a piece of poetry expressing the wonder of ants.*

PLATE V

Ant Garden

Ant gardens high in the canopy of the South American rain forest constitute a complex and sophisticated symbiosis between ants and plants. Ant nests can be as small as a golf ball or as large as a basketball. Ants build the round masses of soil with debris and chewed fibers and pack these around the roots of epiphytic plants to make their nest. Epiphytes are plants that grow above the ground surface using other plants or objects to support their roots and that have evolved in association with ants. Epiphytes need to spread their seeds around hanging gardens. One solution is a sticky seed coating that keeps seeds from falling to the forest floor and that attracts ants. The ants don't eat the seeds but carry them to their nest, where they eat the nutritious coating; the seeds are left to sprout in the nest. As the plants grow, their roots become the framework of the gardens. The ants feed on the nectar provided by the plants. So the ants are planting seeds in these gardens and eating the fruits of their labors, and they build something unique and beautiful, but could be seen as working like farmers.

Actual
1:20

Aztec

1"

PLATE VI

Black and Yellow Argiope ORDER ARANEAE, FAMILY ARANEIDAE, *Argiope aurantia*

These spiders can be found from southern Canada, through the United States, all the way to Costa Rica. As with most spiders, the females are larger than the males, growing to at most a little more than an inch in length. Both sexes have yellow and black markings on their abdomens. To catch insects, they spin an orb web, which is recognized by the zigzag pattern in the middle of the web. The female Argiope built these two papery egg sacs off to the side of the center of the web. In shape, they appear similar to the pots of the potter wasp, although the substance is brown and papery. After the female prepares the egg sacs, she dies. The young spend the winter in the sac and emerge in the spring.

ARTIST'S NOTE: *Some of the wonderful things about the Department of Zoology, Division of Insects, at the Field Museum are the live specimens Jim Louderman, collection assistant, keeps in his office. He has about three dozen tanks, which are not on public display but are used for educational programs. A female Argiope was kept in one of the tanks. Although the species prefers sunny areas among shrubs and flowers, at the Field she lived in a glass tank under a skylight. Liking air movement, she was quite content and comfortable enough to build her little egg sacs. I brought the tank downstairs one Saturday and painted this plate during one of the monthly Artist in the Field programs run by the education department.*

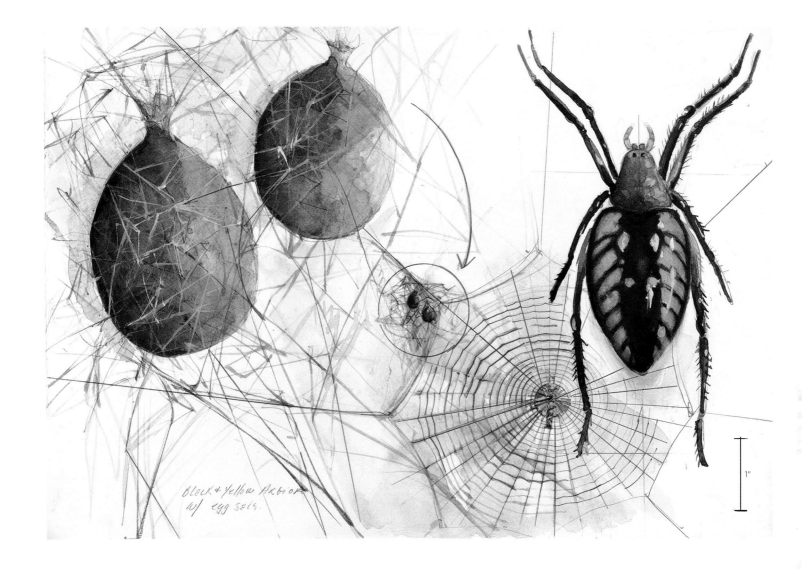

Black & Yellow Arbian
w/ egg sacs.

ARTIST'S NOTE: *This plate was painted from a diorama on display in Animal Kingdom at the Field Museum. It wasn't until I was in Africa in the winter of 2007 that I grasped the full extent of weaver diversity. Their nests were all sizes and shapes, sometimes sprinkled throughout the trees like Christmas ornaments. At other times, they weighed down the branches with nests over a foot in diameter.*

PLATE VII

Village Weaver

ORDER PASSERIFORMES, FAMILY PLOCEIDAE, *Ploceus cucullatus*

A common sight in many African towns, village weavers build large nest colonies or villages, with up to a hundred densely packed nests in a tree. In a wide range of woodlands in river valleys, these nests can be found suspended from thin branches of tall, free-standing trees. Each village weaver male spends from nine to fifteen hours building a handful of nests (from three to five) to attract up to five females. Nests are oval-shaped with a large entrance on the bottom. Each is thick-walled and coarsely woven, with a ceiling of fine leaves. The male begins by forming a woven ring, then builds a chamber and antechamber. Materials include green strips of palm or grass. Females select nests based on structural strength rather than appearance. When a nest is accepted, the male adds an entrance tunnel. The male also strips leaves from branches around each nest. Nests that are not selected are destroyed.

The insert shows another kind of communal weaver nest, that of the sociable weaver, *Philetairus socius*. This bird is slightly bigger than a song sparrow. Pairs build individual nests so near one another that they begin to form a single unit. The community home is extended year after year. As many as 125 flight holes have been counted in these communal nests. One danger of this "apartment complex" approach is that when the group nest becomes too heavy, it falls to the ground.

Village Weaver birds, Ploceus cucullatus.
This weaver-bird gets its name from its
habit of nesting near native villages.
Its own colonies or "villages" sometimes contain 100 nests. The nests
are woven from blades of grass & palm fronds

I 1"

Rupe Wheatcroft
'05

PLATE VIII

Swifts ORDER APODIFORMES, FAMILY APODIDAE

With sickle-shaped wings designed for high-speed flight, swifts are expert flyers, spending most of their time high in the air hunting flying insects. They have been known to sleep on the wing. They resemble swallows, but their nearest relatives are hummingbirds. Their scientific name, Apodidae, means "without feet," but they actually have tiny feet. Their short legs are likely an adaptation for aerodynamics, and their strong claws enable them to perch on the vertical faces of chimneys, caves, rock cliffs, and tree hollows, where they roost and nest.

nest
from

1" nest of
Pew Swift
Cayenne '53

soup

1 Chimney swift

Chaetura pelagica, with nest

Although many of our native North American birds cannot survive in our cities, this swift has adapted to artificial structures, such as chimneys. In this case, human activity actually increased the number of nesting sites. The nest shown here is a half saucer made of dead twigs (plucked in flight) and plant material held together and attached to a flat surface with the bird's hardened saliva. The female lays between three and six eggs. The male shares incubating tasks with the female.

2 White-collared swift

Streptoprocne zonaris

The white-collared swift is a powerful, black bird that resides from Mexico south to Peru. It travels in large flocks of a hundred or more, and often with other swift species. They eat flying insects like beetles, flying ants, and bees on the move. This swift can be seen in the Amazon basin, but it needs caves and cliffs to nest. It builds a saucer-shaped nest of mud, moss, and chitin (insect exoskeletons). A favored nest site is behind waterfalls.

3 Nest of a lesser swallow-tailed swift

Panyptila cayennensis

This medium-sized swift is found from Central to South America in habitats including forest clearings and open woodland. The nest, which takes almost half a year to build, is vertical and tubular, wider at the top, and has an entrance at its base. There is a fake entrance around the center of the tube to fool predators. The nest is made up of plant material and is attached to a branch or vertical surface, like overhanging rock. The eggs are safe in the top of the nest.

4 Swiftlets

Collocalia sp.

The whole swift family is able to bind the sticks of their nests with their own saliva, which dries on contact with the air. The center of this page shows how a group of Southeast Asian swiflets build their nests. They begin by attaching a semicircle of saliva to a flat surface. Then with repeated trips back to the site, they add a bit of saliva each time, raising the rim until a half-open translucent cup is formed. They put their eggs in this cup without padding it. The Asian "edible-nest swiftlet" (*Collocalia fuciphaga*) is named for its valuable pure-saliva nests that are harvested as a delicacy served in soup.

PLATE IX

Wrens ORDER PASSERIFORMES, FAMILY TROGLODYTIDAE

Nests can vary even between related species of the same family. The nests shown here are all made by North American species of wrens in the family Troglodytidae. While these species shared a common ancestor years ago, differences in nest structure reflect both adaptation to different habitats and retention of basic structural similarities (most build domes, or use cavities) that are likely ancestral in the group.

1 Cactus wren

Campylorhynchus brunneicapillus

The cactus wren builds its nest in spiny plants of the North American deserts, such as the thorny acacia bush, tall saguaro cactus, prickly cholla cactus, or yucca. Several nests may be built in a territory, but the wrens breed in only one. In the non-breeding season, additional nests are used for night roosting and shelter from bad weather. All nests are bulky and domed, made of plant fibers, twigs, and dead leaves, and have a side entrance. The final lining is made of fur or feathers.

2 House wren

Troglodytes aedon

All across North America, all kinds of places—cow skulls, flower pots, tin cans, boots, scarecrows, and the pockets of hanging laundry—have been known to harbor house wren nests. They are more often found in natural cavities, tree stumps, woodpecker holes, buildings, and nest boxes. Males begin by building as many as twelve dummy nests, filling prospective nest sites with small sticks. After pairing, the male takes the female to each site and she makes her selection. She then constructs a nest cup from various soft materials, such as feathers, hair, wool, strips of bark, rootlets, moss, and trash.

3 Carolina wren

Thryothorus ludovicianus

Male Carolina wrens of the southeastern United States build multiple nests in their territories, and the females select the final site, with both sexes constructing the ultimate nest. Nests are usually built in enclosed areas: natural cavities, vine tangles, upturned roots, stumps, or abandoned woodpecker holes, but have also been found in nest boxes, mailboxes, glove compartments, tin cans and old shoes. They are rarely more than twelve feet above the ground. It takes from four days to more than a week to build these nests. Domed with a side entrance, they are made from bark strips, dried grasses, dead leaves, sticks, pine needles, mosses, feathers, straw, shed snakeskin, paper, and string, and are lined with hair or fur.

4 Winter wren

Troglodytes troglodytes

The scientific name means "cave-dweller"; the nest is well hidden near the ground, often in exposed roots or in fallen logs in mixed coniferous forest. At night this wren retreats to dark holes and even old woodpecker nests. The winter wren is the only member of the family to occur in the Old World. The male builds up to half a dozen nests near the ground. The female then chooses a nest and lines it with grass, leaves, fine twigs, and moss.

5 Sedge wren

Cistothorus platensis

The sedge wren nest is a round ball of grasses and sedges, with an entrance on the side. The nests are found in dense, tall sedges and grasses in wet meadows, hayfields, and marshes. This secretive species breeds in short grass and sedge marshes, and, with its transitory nesting habits, moves around a great deal from year to year, not staying in one place for long.

6 Rock wren

Salpinctes obsoletus

An interesting characteristic of the rock wren is its creation of a stone walkway, from eight to ten inches long, at the entrance to its nest. It is not clear what purpose the trail serves, but it is built by both genders. Throughout the mountains of western North America rock wren nests can be found on slopes of loose rocks and boulders, in crevices of canyon walls, or sometimes in rodent cavities in banks or tree holes. The nests are well hidden, in spite of their characteristic runways of small stones. Inside the crevice, the wrens construct a foundation of stone. On top of that, the female builds a loose cup of grass, wood, bark, hair, and spider webs, which the male helps bring to the nest.

7 Marsh wren

Cistothorus palustris

Found throughout North American wetlands, the marsh wren's nest is large and round and made of dried grass. Marsh wrens' nests have been seen hanging over small streams, suspended from tree boughs. They are usually found along lake or river borders, among tall reeds such as cattails and bulrushes. These reeds, grasses, or other stems up to a foot long are woven into a hollow ball about seven inches tall and five inches wide. After mating, males accompany the females as they inspect the nests. After selecting one, the female lines it with finer leaves and stems, cattail down and feathers, and constructs a lip at the doorway, extending inward, so that there is a tube entrance.

PLATE X

Osprey ORDER FALCONIFORMES, FAMILY ACCIPITRIDAE, *Pandion haliaetus*

The osprey, or fish hawk, has an almost worldwide distribution and thrives near seacoasts, large lakes, rivers, and estuaries. The species' conspicuous and bulky platform nests can be found in trees or on cliffs, or on offshore structures—such as channel markers, pylons, and duck blinds—near their food supply and, from five to twenty feet high, high enough to protect their young. In North America, they have rebounded from a severe population decline in the 1960s when the pesticide DDT caused the thinning of eggshells, which then would crack during incubation. To encourage recovery, artificial nest platforms were built in many areas. Osprey nests, made of sticks and debris and lined with moss and grass, have a pronounced center depression. In areas of high population density, new breeders must chase away established nesting pairs or settle for a less safe site. When suitable nesting sites are not available, young ospreys may be forced to delay breeding until they find a single bird with an established nest—possibly an older bird whose mate has died.

Osprey
w/ nest

PLATE XI

Pied-billed Grebe ORDER PODICIPEDIFORMES, FAMILY PODICIPEDIDAE, *Podilymbus podiceps*

Together the male and female pied-billed grebe create a floating nest of marsh vegetation that is anchored to plants along the shores of lakes, ponds, and rivers. In many North American wetlands, pied-billed grebes are among the first birds to arrive for spring nesting and last to migrate in the fall, often producing two broods. Nests are usually in the vegetation bordering open water, but they can also rest on the bottom in shallows or between the stems of growing plants. Construction usually takes three to seven days. The nest platform is bulky, with a depression in the center, but very buoyant. Other than during migration, pied-billed grebes seldom fly. If scared, they prefer to escape by diving beneath the water and seeking safety in the reeds. Grebes also use their diving ability to catch their food, preferring fish, frogs, and insects.

PLATE XII

Bald Eagle order falconiformes, family accipitridae, *Haliaeetus leucocephalus*

The nests of the bald eagle are found high in the trees near rivers, lakes, and marshes. These constructions, called aeries, are built to last for years. They are remarkable in size—five to nine feet in diameter—and can weigh two tons! Their shape depends on the nest site. Deep, near-vertical branches call for conical nests; small, upright branches support bowl-shaped structures; and nests on horizontal branches or on the ground take the form of disks. Eagles mate for life and add to and re-use the same nest year after year. New pairs build a nest but don't produce eggs during their first year. During the breeding season, both birds protect a nest territory of one or two square miles from predators and competitors.

PLATE XIII

European White Stork ORDER CICONIIFORMES, FAMILY CICONIIDAE, *Ciconia ciconia ciconia*

European white storks nest in colonies and breed throughout Europe and North Africa. They migrate to Africa during the winter. Upon returning in the spring, the male will enlarge the nest used the previous year, while he waits for the female to arrive. The couple performs a courtship display and often even coo, making gentle sounds, to each other. They are life-long partners. Their nests are huge and bulky. They use available materials, branches, sticks, and debris. Both parents participate in the nest building. The males and females also share incubating the eggs and their care afterward. The young are independent within a couple of months. Their nesting sites are what make this bird unusual. Chimneys, rooftops, tall trees, chimney, and nesting platforms are some of the common locations. Their numbers have decreased because of changes in agricultural practices.

When we know and feel that Nature is our friend, not our implacable enemy . . . then it may be proclaimed that we are on the high-road to a natural and satisfying art, an architecture that will soon become a fine art in the true, the best sense of the word.

LOUIS SULLIVAN, "THE TALL OFFICE BUILDING ARTISTICALLY CONSIDERED"

Paper wasps get their name from the building material they use to construct their nests. They mix macerated wood fibers with their saliva to form the composite material similar to paper. The color of the wasp nest depends on the color of the wood used to make the paper. Some termites use wood particles mixed with saliva or fecal material as a glue to produce a cardboard-like material. Some ant species build nests by mixing wood particles with a sugar solution such as honeydew. These nests are called "carton" nests and can be found in the ground, inside tree cavities, or suspended on the outside of trees.

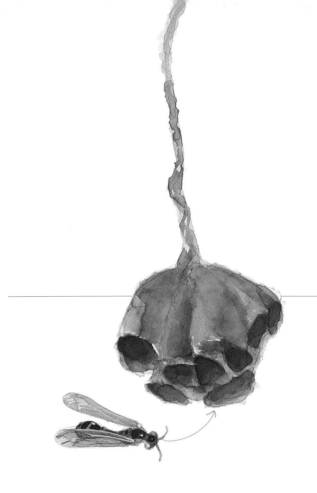

PART TWO

Nests Made of Paper

1–4 *Mischocyttarus*

Mischocyttarus sp.

Mischocyttarus, not as well known as *Polistes*, live primarily in the neotropics, India, and Southeast Asia. A few species are found in North America.

5 *Polistes*

Polistes sp.

The common paper wasps are *Polistes*, which are found worldwide.

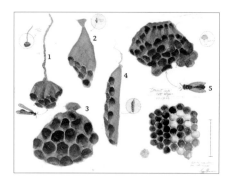

PLATE XIV

Paper Wasp ORDER HYMENOPTERA, FAMILY VESPIDAE, SUBFAMILY POLISTINAE

The two genera illustrated here have similar biology and make nests of open, gray, paper-like cells that hang downward from the underside of a support structure. When searching for a site in the spring, the queen chooses a protected space with overhead cover. She begins the nest by chewing deadwood and mixing it with saliva to form a few cells that hang from a short stalk. Into each cell she lays an egg, and then guards the nest. She feeds the young larvae pieces of chewed caterpillar. After the larvae grow into adults, the newly hatched workers assume the duties of nest building and feeding the next generation of larvae. The size of the adults in the two genera varies, but they are often noticeably smaller than the queen, who stays with the nest to lay more eggs. Nest size varies, because colonies range from six or seven to as many as a hundred individuals. Paper wasp species that live in cold climates hunt caterpillars in late spring and summer. In late summer and fall, nest populations begin to decrease. This is the time when male wasps mate with late-season females, who will overwinter and begin constructing nests in the spring.

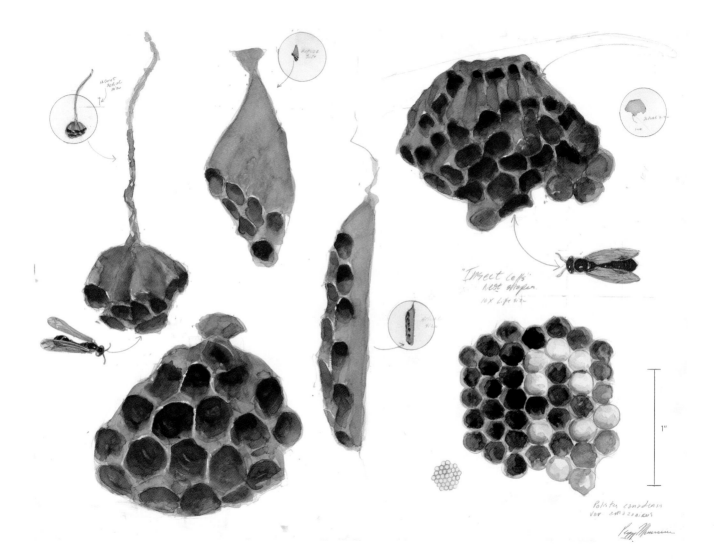

"Insect cells"
Nest shapes
10x life size

Polistes canadensis
var. amazonicus

PLATE XV

Polybia Wasp   ORDER HYMENOPTERA, FAMILY VESPIDAE, *Polybia sericea*

The paper nests of *Polybia sericea* and other species in this genus are produced by groups of queens and workers and are usually oblong or tube-shaped. They are given added stability from the all-around attachment of the combs to the nest cover. The stability comes at a price: there is no room in these nests, generally about eight inches tall, for the wasps to move from story to story. Instead, they build a communication shaft by leaving a hole in the center of each comb. The resulting nests are strong enough to withstand exposure to the elements.

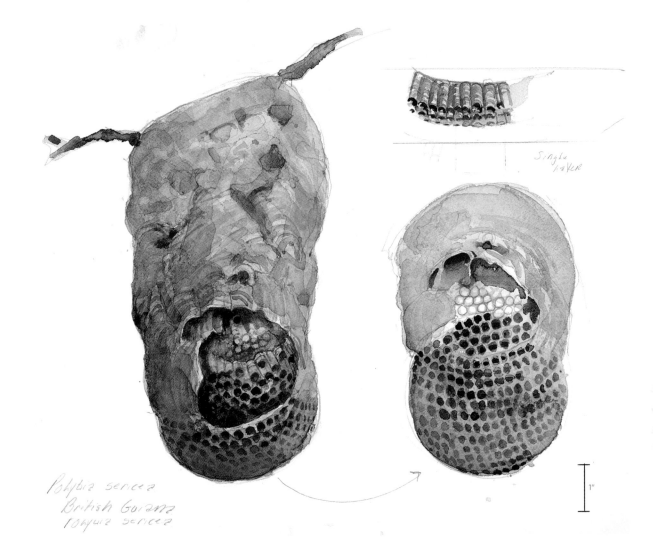

Single
layer

1"

Polybia sericea
British Guiana
Polybia sericea

PLATE XVI

Pasteboard Wasp ORDER HYMENOPTERA, FAMILY VESPIDAE, *Chartergus globiventris*

Chartergus species construct their cylindrical paper nests by adding disc-shaped layers to the base while the top remains securely suspended from a branch. The paper is thick, like 300-lb weight watercolor paper, with a rough surface. The varied color is determined by the different types of wood macerated by the wasps. The nests are made of several stories between eight and nine inches in diameter (shown in insert), and each comb is attached to the outer cover and has a hole in the middle. The central shaft provides communication between the stories of this nest.

1"

PLATE XVII

Wasp Nest in Palm   ORDER HYMENOPTERA, FAMILY VESPIDAE, *Protopolybia* sp.

This nest was built by a South American wasp, *Protopolybia* sp. About fourteen inches tall, the nest is a series of vertical combs on top of each other. These tiny, perfectly formed layers of combs are wrapped up in a thin paper. The palm in this case serves as the backing for the nest. When the leaf dies it will turn a similar color to the nest and help hide it in the habitat.

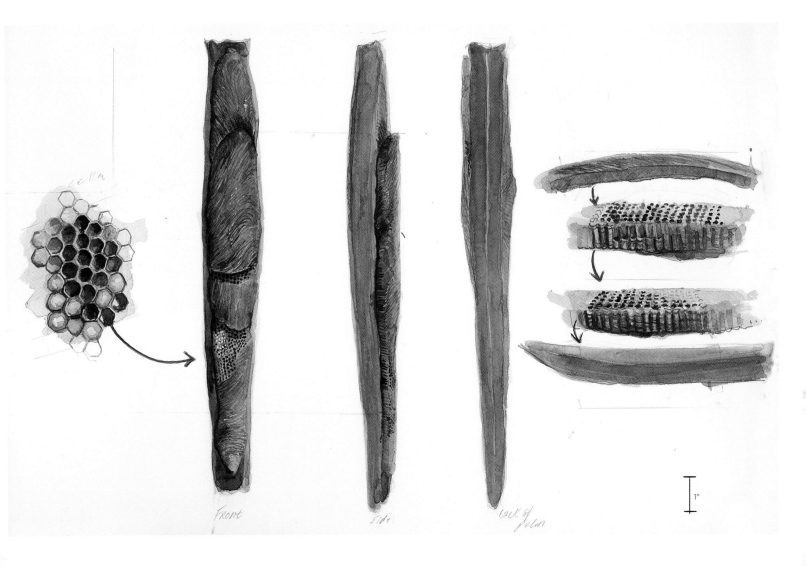

cera

Front

side

back of
palm

1"

PLATE XVIII

Ant Nests

ORDER HYMENOPTERA, FAMILY FORMICIDAE

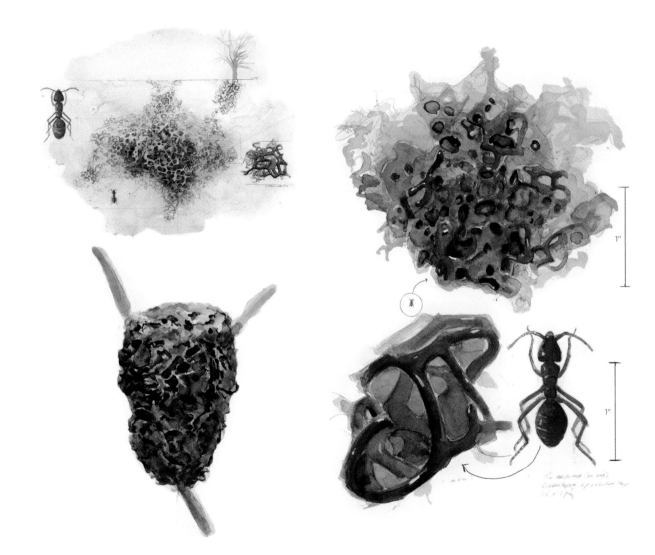

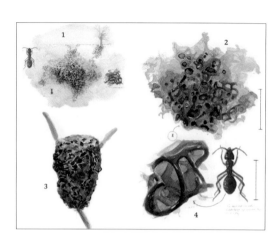

1, 2, 4 *Liometopum apiculatum*   **3 *Crematogaster***

The ant *Liometopum apiculatum* is found in the foothills of the south-western United States and Mexico where it constructs carton nests in the ground. The nest shown in the illustration is about twelve inches long and eight inches in diameter and strong enough to be lifted as a whole. *Liometopum* species will sometimes start the construction of their nest at the base of a tree then expand down and out, underground, away from the tree. This specimen illustrates the inside of the nest with all the tunnels and galleries that make up the labyrinth constructed by the colony of worker ants.

The *Crematogaster* species makes a carton nest on trees. About ten inches in height, the nest is a black irregular mass of tunnels and openings. This species infuses bits of chewed wood with a concentrated sugar solution as a binding agent for the carton. The carton is made in flakes and is laid like shingles to allow rain to run off the nest. The nest pictured here was found in India.

Architecture is the learned game, correct and magnificent, of forms assembled in the light.

LE CORBUSIER

Mud is used mostly by two insect orders, Isoptera, the termites, and Hymenoptera, the bees, wasps, and ants. The majority of the huge termite mounds are composed of mud mixed with saliva. The potter wasps and mud daubers are examples of Hymenoptera that use mud to build their nests. Fewer than 5 percent of bird species use mud as a building material. The flamingos use only mud to build their nests. The cliff swallows utilize mud mixed with grass to create tension so as to suspend their nests from cliffs or overhanging rocks.

PART THREE

Nests Made of Mud

PLATE XIX

Mud Nests

1 Greater flamingo

Order Ciconiiformes, family Phoenicopteri-
dae, *Phoenicopterus ruber*

The greater flamingo of Africa and
the New World tropics needs shallow,
very salty coastal lagoons, mudflats,
and lakes in which to feed and breed
successfully. Flamingos will often
seek out large expanses of shallow
water for protection, as they dis-
like disturbance, especially during
breeding season. Males and females
build the nest together. The nest is
a flattened cone made of mud and
bits of vegetation measuring about
twelve to twenty inches in diameter
and eighteen inches in height. There
is a shallow depression on top for the
female's single egg (occasionally there
are two). Despite the circular trench
constructed around this mound, the
nest and egg are frequently destroyed
by rising water levels.

2 Cliff swallow

Order Passeriformes, family Hirundinidae,
Petrochelidon pyrrhonota

In natural settings like overhangs on
cliffs or on bridges and other artificial
structures, cliff swallows breed in
colonies that can range from a few
to hundreds of nests. The male and
female build the nest together, usually
taking one to two weeks. They collect
mud in ponds, puddles, and ditches
as much as a half mile away. Each nest
contains 1,000 to 1,400 pellets of mud,
silt, and clay; each pellet represents
a trip from the nest and back again.
Nests are conical or gourd-shaped, enclosed structures with an exit tunnel
that slopes downward. The interior
is lined sparingly with grasses, hair,
and feathers. Hematophagous (blood-
sucking) insects and mites are a big
problem for swallows. Infestations
of swallow bugs (Oeciacus vicarious)
cause up to half of all nestling deaths.
They spread rapidly by crawling from
nest to nest or by clinging to feathers
of adult birds and can survive in unoc-
cupied nests without food for as long
as three years. In selecting a nest site,
cliff and barn swallows apparently

assess which nests are heavily infested with parasites and avoid them. The birds will even prematurely desert their nests en masse, leaving their young to starve, when swallow bug populations become too great.

ARTIST'S NOTE: *For one month I observed a colony of cliff swallows as they built nests on the modern buildings on Northwestern University's lakefront campus.*

3 Ovenbird nest

(See text on plate XX.)

4 Potter Wasp

(See text on plate XXI.)

PLATE XX

Ovenbirds

ORDER PASSERIFORMES, FAMILY FURNARIIDAE

White-throated Treerunner
Pygarrhichas albogularis
+ Asthenes spinstail
Synallaxis azarae (sp?)
Ovenbirds
Family Furnariidae

1"

1 Azara's spinetail

Synallaxis azarae

This species and those that follow are members of a large family of insectivorous birds native to South and Central America. Some members of this family, such as this spinetail, build domed grass nests, but other members of the family, such as tree-hunters (*Thripadectes* spp., tree hole) and horneros (mud dome) build such a variety of nests that scientists have used this variation in trying to recon-struct evolutionary relationships in the family.

2 Rufous horneo

Furnarius rufus

In a wide variety of open habitats across South America, both male and female rufous horneros participate in the building of the nest, taking about two weeks. Their building instincts are awakened by hormones. The birds carry about two thousand small lumps of clay to the branch or other chosen building site. Using their beaks and feet, they mold the spheri-cal nest, mixing vegetable debris and feces with the clay to hold it together. An antechamber leads to a large brooding area that is padded with fine grass. About five weeks after the eggs are laid, the young birds are ready to leave the nest. They do not return because the nest becomes as hot as an oven in the tropical summer sun.

3 White-throated treerunner
Pygarrhichas albogularis

The white-throated treerunner of the *Nothofagus* (false beech) forests of southern South America has strikingly convergent habits to nuthatches of the northern hemisphere, including being able to move downward on tree trunks. They forage by gleaning insects from the bark and leaf petioles of trees. Treerunners make their nests in rotten trunks or partially burned wood, using the sawdust from their own work and dry straw for lining.

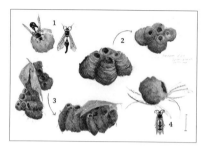

PLATE XXI

Potter Wasps ORDER HYMENOPTERA, FAMILY VESPIDAE, SUBFAMILY EUMENINAE

The inch-long adult female potter wasp builds a nest out of mud that resembles a little pot. To make the nest she presses the mud with her mandibles and front legs into pellets. Carrying the pellets to the nest site, she constructs the nest by flattening the pellets to form the exterior. After the nest is built, the wasp collects enough beetle or moth larvae to allow her offspring to feed until it pupates. She forces the stunned prey inside the nest. As she lays the egg, she secretes a strand of sticky fluid that suspends it safely above the paralyzed prey so the egg doesn't get crushed when the prey wakes up. After she lays her egg she seals the nest with one last strip of mud and then has nothing to do with the offspring. Not all Eumeninae species use mud to make their pot-like nests. Some species in the genus Zethus use chewed leaves and sap to construct their nests.

Trial blocks #59
Euclurus globalis
Bottes nest

1"

PLATE XXII

Mud Daubers

ORDER HYMENOPTERA, FAMILY SPHECIDAE

1 Organ pipe mud dauber

Order Hymenoptera, family Sphecidae,
subfamily Crabroninae, *Trypoxylon* sp.

The adult organ pipe mud dauber
is black and shiny and about three-
quarters of an inch in length. Its long,
slender nest can be found attached to
a roof or overhang or under an eave.
The day after a summer rain, this
sphecid wasp gathers mud from the
edge of puddles, forms it into tubes,
and arranges the tubes next to each
other like organ pipes. Each "pipe"
contains an implanted single egg and
several paralyzed spiders (top left).
Once they hatch, the young feed on
the spiders. The males may guard the
nest while the females hunt for food.

2 Black and yellow mud dauber

Order Hymenoptera, family Sphecidae,
subfamily Sphecinae, *Sceliphron* sp.

The subfamily Sphecinae or thread-
waisted wasps are very common. The
North American species of the black
and yellow mud daubers construct
nests similar to the organ pipe mud
dauber except that each cell is only
about 25 millimeters in length, which
is much shorter than the organ pipe
cell. These wasps supply each cell
with spiders. Some species found in
the neotropics construct nests made
up of a series of cylindrical cells that
are plastered over by small bits of
mud to form a smooth nest as large as
two inches in diameter.

1"

1 **Cross section of the nest**
2 **Nest with insect**

PLATE XXIII

Polybia Wasp ORDER HYMENOPTERA, FAMILY VESPIDAE, *Polybia emaciata*

This species of polybia builds nests about six inches tall, with the outer cover consisting of a mortar made from clay and sand. The topmost comb is attached to a branch by a stem; a further support connects it to the domed top of the mortar cover. The lower combs are not joined together by supports as are those of hornets and their relations—they are attached to the sides of the outer cover. Instead of a central communication or flight shaft, a gap is left between combs and cover in the region of the flight hole, allowing wasps to move from comb to comb.

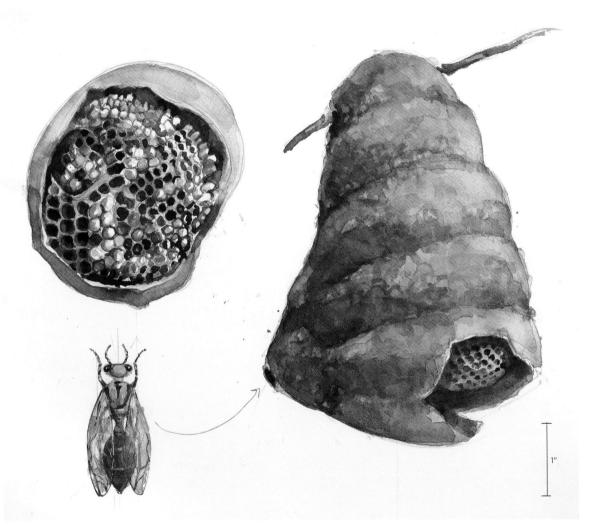

1"

The best way to make real architecture is by letting a building evolve out of the culture and place. These small projects designed by students at the studio remind us what it means to have an American architecture without pretense. They offer us a simple glimpse into what is essential to the future of American architecture, its honesty.

SAMUEL MOCKBEE

Mounds range from the simple nest of the Sandhill Crane, which is just above the ground, to the complicated African termite nest, which rises up each in its own unique, undulating shape, to the complicated constructions of the bowerbird, who decorates with just about anything to attract his mate. These nests are built to blend in with the environment. By using readily available material, the animal both recycles and disguises its nest. The digger wasp nest, although just a "hole in the ground," is an example of simple, safe housing. Termites, in addition to producing large broods to ensure the continuation of the species, also protect the brood by hiding them within the large mound. The civil engineering involved in these mounds is simple and an environmentally sound example for us all.

PART FOUR

Nests Made by Depressions and Mounds

PLATE XXIV

Mound Builders

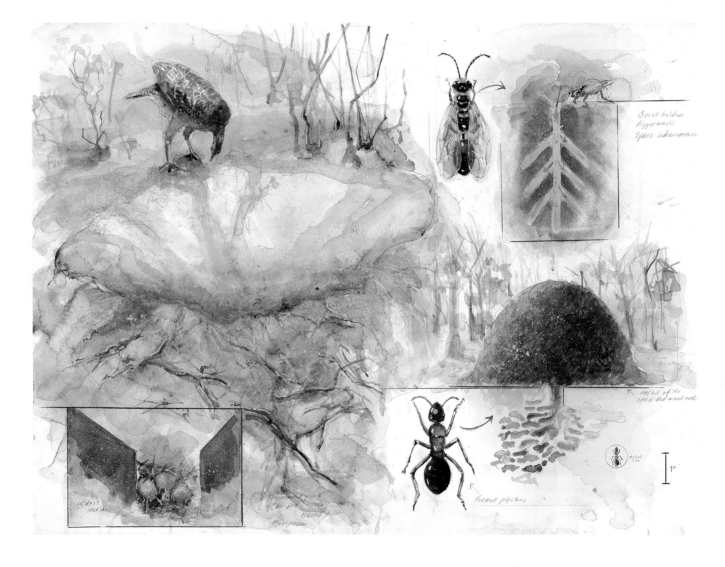

Great Golden
Digger and
Sphex ichneumoneus

Ant hill of the
south-Red wood ant

Cross
section

Formica polyctena

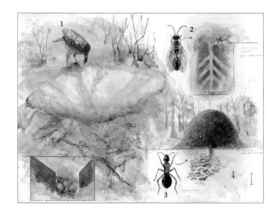

1 Malleefowl

Order Galliformes, family Megapodiidae, *Leipoa ocellata*

The megapodes, or mound builders, including the malleefowl, are a group of Old World chicken-like birds from eastern Indonesia, New Guinea, and Australia with a peculiar nest-building habit: they do not incubate the eggs with body heat like other birds, but bury them in large nest mounds of sand and compost. Building begins in April or May and both genders participate. They start by digging a large hole about 1 meter (about 3.3 feet) in depth. They fill the hole with vegetable material and sand to form a mound. Eggs are laid in August. The adults spend most of the year tending to the temperature of the interior, checking it daily, removing material to warm the eggs and adding material to keep them cool. After all this work the chicks hatch already feathered and tunnel up to the surface of the mound. There is no further parental care—the chicks simply wander away and fend for themselves.

2 Great golden digger wasp

Order Hymenoptera, family Sphecidae, sub-family Sphecinae, *Sphex ichneumoneus*

The great golden digger wasp is found in the United States and southern Canada and south into the tropics. The female wasp digs a vertical tunnel in hard-packed soil of sandy meadows; several more tunnels radiate from the initial tunnel. The female paralyzes her prey of crickets and long-horned grasshoppers, drags them down to a cell, and lays one egg on each victim. As she digs these burrows and throws the excavated soil behind, she creates the mound.

3 Small red wood ant

Order Hymenoptera, family Formicidae,
Formica polyctena

Digging tunnels underground is the
first step in nest building for small
red wood ants. The ants may begin
the nest in a tree stump; the workers
hollow out passages and chambers
underground. They then work on
the openings that lead to the outside.
To cover these they collect needles,
twigs, bits of moss, grass, and lichen
and start the construction of a large
mound. They continue to work both
above and below ground. The ants are
constantly carrying nesting material
from the lower strata to the surface
and covering the outside of the nest.
The mound is similar to a thatched
roof, which sheds water and can be
over three feet high and six feet wide.

ARTIST'S NOTE: *My favorite bowerbird story is that of the orange-crested gardener (Amblyornis subalaris). The male actually builds a kind of hut on the forest floor, complete with a waterproof roof. He covers the center of the façade with dark green moss; here on the "canvas" the bird arranges his treasures. On the left might be his shiny insect collection and to the right some shells. Then the bird gathers small flowers and creates a colorful line through the center. As the bird brings more elements to the installation, he actually steps back and observes the final "composition." If dissatisfied, the bowerbird adjusts the flowers ever so slightly. But even the best art does not insure love and attention. When the bowerbird is finally graced with a female visitor, he still has to dance and display his flashy red crest. (From Heinz Sielmann, Lockende Wildnis: Das Reich der Drachen und Zaubervögel [Gütersloh: Bertelsmann Sachbuchverlag, 1970]; cited in Karl von Frisch's Animal Architecture.)*

PLATE XXV

Fawn-breasted Bowerbird ORDER PASSERIFORMES, FAMILY PTILONORHYNCHIDAE, *Chlamydera cerviniventris*

In tropical forests in northern Australia and New Guinea, the male fawn-breasted bowerbird builds an elaborate grass tunnel or bower to attract the female. Although not a nest, this bower, used just for mating, is a wonderful example of construction. The male decorates the entrance with a collection of like objects that are carefully collected, sorted, and arranged by color. This entrance often includes hundreds of shells, bones, leaves and flowers, stones, or berries. The male eats green plants and paints the walls with saliva and plant paste. The female chooses the male who, in her eyes, decorates the most exciting bower.

In the larger bowerbird family there is a tendency for the more colorful species to build less elaborate bowers. The fawn-breasted bowerbird is a dull brown bird that builds an intricate structure, involving an extensive platform of twigs that includes the main bower. Actual nests are constructed by females at some distance from the bower. They are simple platforms of twigs in the forest. The female then incubates the eggs and raises the chicks.

PLATE XXVI

Sandhill Crane   ORDER GRUIFORMES, FAMILY GRUIDAE, *Grus canadensis*

These distinctively long-legged gray birds with red foreheads are the beautiful sandhill cranes. They frequent marshes feeding on frogs, fish, and insects, but also can be seen in fields feeding on grain. Breeding across parts of the northern United Sates and Canada, they migrate to the American South for the winter, returning each spring. Huge flocks stop over at the Platte River in Nebraska to feed and rest on their journey. Shying away from human interference, cranes build solitary nests of plant matter, creating a low mound in a marsh or on ground near water. Following a long decline, overall breeding numbers in some areas such as Wisconsin are recovering.

PLATE XXVII

Game Birds

1 Ring-necked pheasant

Order Galliformes, family Phasianidae, sub-family Phasianinae, *Phasianus colchicus*

The female ring-necked pheasant shown here is far less showy than her male counterpart. The nest is built on the ground, between April and June, in tall grass or weeds, using a scrape in ground or vegetation. The nest is unlined or sparsely lined with plant material, and occasionally a few breast feathers from the female. It holds about ten eggs.

2 Wild turkey

Order Galliformes, family Meleagridae, *Meleagris gallopavo*

In oak woodland, pine oak forest, open forest, and wooded swamps, wild turkeys huddle together. The male spreads his magnificent tail feathers to form a fan and struts around his territory waiting for the hens. Ten or more hens will mate with one tom, and then each will leave to build its nest in safety. Nests are shallow depressions lined with grass and leaves and hidden in a forested area. Hens lay one egg a day for eight to twenty days. They guard their nests during the day and roost in trees at night. After being hunted almost to extinction, these birds have made a strong comeback throughout their North American range.

3 Northern bobwhite, with nest
Order Galliformes, family Odontophoridae,
Colinus virginianus

Bobwhite quails are stout little game
birds and can be heard calling their
name, "Bob-white, Bob-white." They
live as couples during the breeding
season in open woodlands, fields, and
meadows of eastern North America.
When not breeding, northern bob-
whites live together in coveys of
eight to twenty-five birds. Both sexes
choose the breeding site and work
at building the nest. Two or three
females will share a nest if the species is abundant and there isn't much
cover for safety. The nests are shallow,
saucer-shaped depressions that are
scraped into the ground, lined with
grass, moss, and pine needles. These
constructions are hidden in weeds or
grass, fifty feet from a clearing. Bob-
whites and other quail can lay up to
eighteen eggs each season. This is one
of the largest clutch sizes of any bird.

PLATE XXVIII

Emu, Tinamou, and Kiwi

1 Emu

Order Casuariiformes, family Dromaiidae, *Dromaius novaehollandiae*

The emu nest is a shallow ground platform of grass near shrubbery, on the grassy plains and dry open forests of Australia. It is formed from leaves, grasses, and bark and is about ten centimeters high (about four inches) and one to two meters in diameter (about three to six feet). It holds fifteen to twenty-five eggs, which come from several hens. Nesting takes place in winter. The male and female remain together for a few months, including courtship, nest building, and egg laying. The female dominates during pair formation, but once incubation begins the male drives away other emus, including his mate. The male sits on the nest for fifty-five days without leaving for any reason, including eating, drinking, and elimination. Eggs can roll out of the nest and are pulled back in by the male.

2 Southern kiwi or tokoeka

Order Apterygiformes, family Apterygidae, *Apteryx australis*

By night, Kiwis hunt on the forest floor for food; by day they roost in ground cavities or under tree roots near their nests. Kiwis may occupy many dens and nesting burrows by rotation throughout their territory, which is marked by feces, a trait more in common with mammals than with other birds. They sniff out food and have whiskers and scent glands. Not surprisingly, the kiwi has been called the bird world's "honorary mammal." Kiwis are found only in New Zealand and are the only survivors of an ancient order of birds that includes the now-extinct moas. Kiwis are unique in that the females have two functional ovaries; in all other species of birds, females have only one working ovary. They also hold the record for laying the largest egg in relationship to body size. Each of the one to three eggs the female lays weighs about 25 percent of her total weight. Kiwis breed during the southern winter, during which time they form pair bonds. The male excavates a burrow or digs a hole under a tree and the female lays her eggs at it's end. The male does all the incubation, which takes seventy-eight to eighty-two days. The young are not fed for the first few days of their lives because although they are precocial, there is so much yolk in the eggs that they are born with plenty of food reserves.

3 Head of Greater Rhea

Order Struthioniformes, family Rheidae, *Rhea americana*

Rheas are the South American relative of the ostrich, and on the pampas and other grasslands they fulfill a similar ecological niche, feeding mainly on vegetation, but taking insects and small vertebrates when possible. There are two species of rhea. The greater or common rhea, *Rhea americana*, is the larger of the two and stands about 1.6 meters (5 feet) high and weighs about twenty-five kilograms (pounds). Males choose a territory near some water and scrub and make a nest there. Rheas are another example of the males taking on most of the work. They build the nest as well as incubate the young after the females lay the eggs. In addition, the males are fierce protectors of the nest.

4 Elegant crested tinamou

Order Tinamiformes, family Tinamidae, *Eudromia elegans*

The crested tinamou inhabits open country from Brazil to central Argentina. It is distantly related to running birds like the emu and kiwi. It inhabits agricultural land, where it eats insects and ticks that are present around cattle. It also can be found in the scrub and savannah. Its nest is a shallow depression lined with sticks and grasses. The eggs are a gray-green color with a beautiful enamel-like sheen. In this species, the mating system is polygynandry, where males and females mate with multiple partners. The males incubate and care for the young.

5 Great tinamou

Order Tinamiformes, family Tinamidae, *Tinamus major*

This well-camouflaged bird can be found in the rain forests of central and South America. If you can't see it, you definitely will recognize its distinctive call of four loud, haunting notes. The female builds the nest on the ground with bits of bark scraped off the tree roots. The male does all the childcare while the female goes off and mates again. She may have as many as half a dozen nests during one eight-month breeding season.

ARTIST'S NOTE: *My inspiration for this illustration came from a three-dimensional diorama at the Field Museum of a giant anteater and termite mound from Brazil. The original watercolor is forty by sixty inches, to accommodate this large nest and the giant anteater.*

PLATE XXIX

Termite Mound

ORDER ISOPTERA, FAMILY TERMITIDAE, *Macrotermes* sp.

Termites have a bad reputation, but they are very important to ecosystems. They are valuable recyclers, contributing to the decomposition process. They eat mainly dead wood that other organisms can't. A *Macrotermes* mound can reach a height of 3 to 4 meters (about 9.8 to 13 feet) and support a population of two million termites. To regulate the temperature of their nest, termites create an air conditioning system. Air enters tunnels built on the side of the nest and escapes through the top. The inside is made up of foraging tunnels as well as galleries for immature nymphs, the queen, and other adult termites. These mounds can be invaded by driver ants (genus *Dorylus*), also known as army ants. The ants enter where the building is soft, at the top. They easily overtake the termites because they are more agressive. Often the worker termites hide in the royal chamber, so the termite colony continues.

The giant anteater, *Myrmecophaga tridactyla*, can be found in grasslands, savannahs, and rain forests of South America. It feasts on ants and termites, with a long snake-like tongue that, once the termite nest is broken into, serves to lick up the eggs, immature nymphs, and grown insects.

PLATE XXX

Termites

1 Compass termites

Order Isoptera, family Termitidae, *Amitermes meridionalis*

Inhabitants of the Australian steppe, compass termites build flat wall structures that are up to 5 meters high and 3 meters long (about 16 feet high and 9.8 feet long). The two narrow sides face north and south so that their exposure to the midday sun is minimal. The long, flat sides catch the weaker morning and evening sun, so the nest does not overheat. The fact that worker termites are blind makes their nest-building feat even more remarkable.

2 Black mound termite

Order Isoptera, family Termitidae, *Amitermes atlanticus*

Black mound termites, like compass termites, build multiple nests near one another. They are numerous in places where the soil is sandy. The largest mound is only about two feet high and two feet in diameter. Because these termites use their excrement as the outer layer, their nests are black. This layer dries hard and fast like cement and deters intruders. The mounds extend underground and the termites are able to communicate with one another by circular openings about one-sixteenth of an inch in diameter.

3 Arboreal termite nest

Order Isoptera, family Termitidae, *Nasutitermes* sp.

The most familiar form of the termite nest is the mound, but some species in the genus *Nasutitermes* build carton nests in trees. It is hard to distinguish these arboreal carton nests from those of the ant genus *Crematogaster* (see plate XVIII). The best way to determine the architect is to examine the specimens inhabiting the nest.

4 Roofed mounds

Order Isoptera, family Termitidae, *Cubitermes* sp.

Roofs with overhangs on tall, thin mounds characterize the nests of certain species of the genus *Cubitermes*. The termites have built roofs that protect the structure from the torrential rains. In arid zones, the same species does not add the roof, showing that they are used as umbrellas, not sunscreens.

5 Underground nest

Order Isoptera, family Termitidae, *Apicotermes gurgulifex*

This underground termite builds a nest with an air space around it, which helps alleviate ventilation problems. The floors of the layered nest are joined by a central path. The outer wall of rings shows consistent workmanship. This species uses its quickly drying excreta to fashion this miniature work of art.

PLATE XXXI

Fungus Garden   ORDER ISOPTERA, FAMILY MACROTERMITIDAE

Cultivation of *Basidiomycete* fungi in specially prepared underground chambers is practiced by the fungus-growing termites in the family Macrotermitidae. Termite feces are used to nurture the fungus gardens (top center), which the termites are nutritionally dependent upon. In many Macrotermitidae communities, the king and queen are concealed in a narrow cell known as the royal chamber, where only the smaller workers can enter and leave. The queens in some *Macrotermes* species have enlarged abdomens that can grow up to 14 centimeters long and 3.5 centimeters wide (5.5 by 1.3 inches). These queens have enormous ovaries and can lay a thousand eggs or more a day. Queens live for several years. The sexually productive king and queen can be replaced when they die. The colony and their structure are able to last for decades.

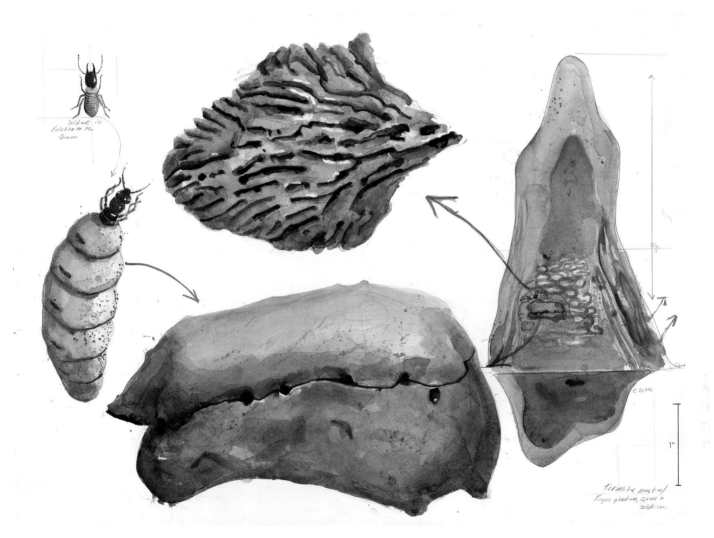

Soldier in
relation to the
Queen

Termite nest w/
fugus garden, queen &
soldiers

Organic architecture includes all materials, accepts all forms so they be natural to purpose, considerate of ways and means and respectful to environment. . . . Wood, as we may now see, is patterned, textured in endless variety by the inherent nature of effervescence and, obeying the law of the crystals, achieving color, textures, patterns, endless in beauty, perfect in point of style.

FRANK LLOYD WRIGHT, "ON ARCHITECTURE"

These nests are made in wood. Their makers are a natural example of Wright's 'organic architecture.' They use what is there, manipulating it for their own uses, but also participating in the natural cycle. While the woodpecker works an old tree to a smooth hollow, others use an existing hollow to secure their young. Some woodpeckers use the shavings from their carving to line the nest, thereby using the medium to its fullest extent with little waste. The hornbills take the extra step of sealing the female and her eggs into the hollow. Carpenter ants create their home and nest by tunneling into soft decaying wood. The resulting structure is a molded sculpture both functional and beautiful. The fact that it also helps to further the decay of the stump is a wonderful side benefit to the larger natural picture.

PART FIVE

Nests Made by Carving Wood

PLATE XXXII

Wood Carvers

1 Black carpenter ant

Order Hymenoptera, family Formicidae, *Camponotus herculeanus*

Black carpenter ants can be found throughout the world and use tree trunks for nesting places. They prefer partially decayed trees because they are easier for them to tunnel into. The nest is built according to the tree's annual rings. The concentric layers of wood are differentiated by a lighter area grown in the spring and a darker (tougher) outer section. In order to dig out their chambers, carpenter ants tunnel through the softer areas and leave the hard parts.

2 Rhinoceros hornbill

Order Coraciiformes, family Bucerotidae, *Buceros rhinoceros*

Hornbills like this rhinoceros hornbill are large birds of the Old World tropics that nest in the hollows of trees. The male, shown here at the nest, has a large, protuberant casque on top of the bill. These birds eat fruit and insects and have a harsh, penetrating call. When ready to lay, the female enters the chosen nest cavity, where she will remain for many weeks. Once inside, she makes a substance of soil (brought by the male), saliva, excreta, and food residue. She plasters this mass around the opening of her nest, leaving only a small slit. Throughout the incubation and nesting period, the male brings food to the female and later the female and the young, passing it though the slit. As the chicks grow larger, the mother eventually breaks down this wall to go out and help feed them. The young renew the wall themselves and break out in stages. Studies have shown the logging in their native Southeast Asia has reduced the overall numbers of rhinoceros hornbills, but even after the surrounding forest has been disturbed, pairs will try to return to their customary nest sites.

3 Red-headed woodpecker

Order Piciformes, family Picidae, *Melanerpes erythrocephalus*

The red-headed woodpecker can be found east of the Rockies and west of New England. They are most common in the Midwest's open forests. They nest in dead trees and have to compete with starlings for these sites. Dead trees are often cut down, and this has decreased the number of nesting sites. Red-headed woodpeckers eat a variety of foods; besides insects, they also eat corn and cultivated fruit. They find empty holes and crevices, and store food like acorns and beechnuts for the winter, then place a piece of bark to cover the hole. It takes the males about two weeks to excavate the nesting site.

4 Northern flicker

Order Piciformes, family Picidae, *Colaptes auratus*

Dead trees and stumps are the preferred nesting places of the common flicker throughout North America. Both genders help excavate a cavity that is ten to ninety feet above the ground, a task that takes from one to three weeks. A natural cavity saves the birds the effort of creating their own. Wood chips left at the bottom of the space cushion the eggs. Both parents are active in incubating the eggs and caring for their young.

PLATE XXXIII

Woodpeckers

ORDER PICIFORMES, FAMILY PICIDAE

1 Northern three-toed woodpecker
Picoides tridactylus

This bird inhabits boreal forests of New England, New York, and Northern Wisconsin and throughout Canada to Alaska. The entrance to the nest is an irregular opening, less than two inches wide and about two inches high. The nest has a depth of about one foot.

2 Pileated woodpecker
Dryocopus pileatus

A new hole is excavated annually by this woodpecker. The oval or oblong entrance has a diameter of about three inches, and the nest can be as much as twenty-four inches deep. The finished product is the work of both the male and female. This species is widespread across all of eastern North America and reaches the west coast locally in Washington and southern Canada.

3 Ivory-billed woodpecker
Campephilus principalis

The magnificent ivory-billed woodpecker of southeastern forests was believed to be extinct; however, the controversy continues about its possible survival. Ornithologists searched for the bird and its nest in the areas where recent sightings were reported. Field Museum scientists were among the groups sent to Arkansas for the search. Stay tuned for the outcome.

4 Downy woodpecker
Picoides pubescens

The downy woodpecker is the most common woodpecker in much of eastern North America and very similar in coloration and pattern to the larger hairy woodpecker. The female chooses the nesting site and the male does most of the carpentry work.

5 Hairy woodpecker
Dendrocopos villosus

The hairy woodpecker, which is found throughout North America, builds a nest with an entrance hole 2.5 inches high and 2 inches wide. The interior cavity is about a foot long and a foot wide at the base. Both the male and female work to build the nest, which takes them about three weeks. They prepare a new nesting cavity every year. Three to four eggs are laid at the base on wood chips. The courtship can begin in February, three months before the breeding season in April. Both the male and female guard the young. The male often takes the watch at night.

ARTIST'S NOTE: *A friend noticed a birch tree had been cut down in her neighborhood. As she examined the fallen tree, she noticed a woodpecker nest, which now rests proudly in my home. The entrance is a perfect oval hole into which I can put three fingers. The inside is very smooth, as if it were sanded. Then the nest expands and heads downward. When you look at the entrance, it blends into the other markings of the tree.*

PLATE XXXIV

Carpenter Ants in Aspen Stump ORDER HYMENOPTERA, FAMILY FORMICIDAE, *Camponotus* sp.

At the left in plate XXXII, the illustration shows a tree trunk cut vertically, and you can see how the ant hollowed along the lines of the tree's annual rings. In this example, however, the hollowed areas are horizontal, across the grain. The walls of the galleries are smooth, as if they had been sandpapered. The insects remove these shavings and carry them outside the nest. They do not actually eat the wood, but simply create galleries to rear their young.

ARTIST'S NOTE: *When I pulled this specimen out of its shoebox and removed the wrapping paper, I felt I was looking at a model for a design by the Spanish architect Antonio Gaudi, whose organic style and fluid lines created dreamlike architecture.*

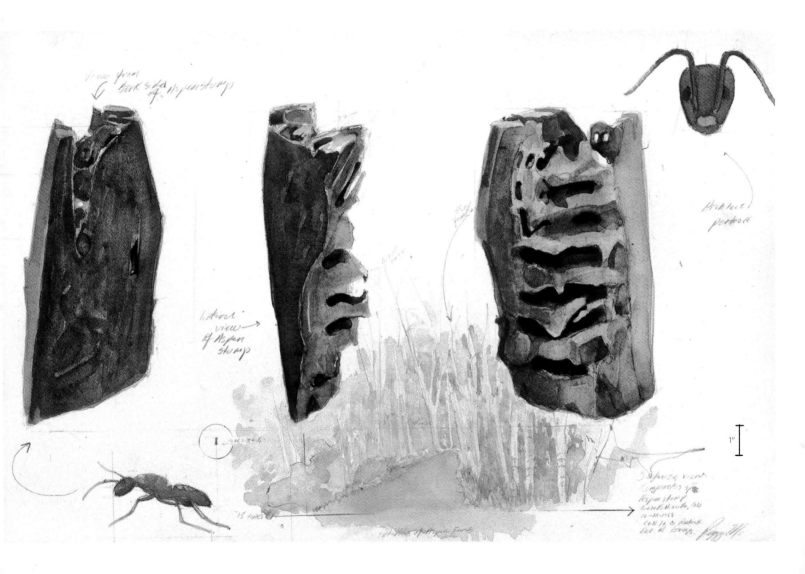

view from bark side of Aspen stump

lateral view of Aspen stump

Architect portrait

1"

Architecture should speak of its time and place but yearn for timelessness.
                                                                    FRANK GEHRY

All seasons provide the chance for the budding naturalist of any age to observe nest building. It requires no equipment, just careful observation and listening. During the springtime breeding season, it is often apparent that a nest is nearby, even if it cannot be seen. A frantic adult warns you off with sharp sounds or even attacks, if you get too close, and the nest stays hidden. Other nests are brought to your attention by the sound of the young calling for their share of the food. We see the adults flitting in and out of a large shrub as they attend their young. In summer you can observe the patience of the cliff swallow as it brings bits of sand and mud back to its globular nest plastered to a building. As autumn leaves fall to the ground a vast array of animal and insect homes that were hidden away in summer greenery are revealed. And finally winter can be a time to collect that abandoned hornet's nest or a robin's nest that has fallen to the ground.

PART SIX

Nests Found Close to Home

PLATE XXXV

Cardinal, Red-winged Blackbird, Brown-headed Cowbird, and Meadowlark

1 Northern cardinal

Order Passeriformes, family Cardinalidae, *Cardinalis cardinalis*

Northern cardinals mate for life. They feed together over the winter and sing together in spring, one bird beginning the song and the other completing it. The female builds the nest, which seems small and fragile for a bird of this size. The nest is above ground and made of stems, twigs, and bark strips. Both the male and female feed the young and have as many as four broods in a season.

2, 3 Red-winged blackbird

Order Passeriformes, family Icteridae, *Agelaius phoeniceus*

Like many migratory birds, male red-winged blackbirds (3) arrive on the breeding ground first, heralding the coming of spring with their loud advertising calls designed to attract females.The females (2) build the nest, making a cup of grass, attached to reeds or hidden in a hedgerow. Males vigorously defend the area around the nest (lower right), often dive-bombing perceived intruders, including human passersby.

4 Brown-headed cowbird

Order Passeriformes, family Icteridae, *Molothrus ater*

Shown in the drawing under the female red-winged blackbird is a cowbird leaving her eggs in other birds' nests. It has been reported that there are as many as 220 host species for brown-headed cowbirds. The cowbird's eggs are very similar to that of the cardinal and the red-winged blackbird, oval with brown spots. (The cardinal's egg spots are more

plentiful, and the red-wing blackbird's eggs are pale blue and marked
with lines and dots.) The cowbird usually lays only one egg in the host nest
and manages to pass on her mothering duties to other birds, preferably
warblers, vireos, and finches.

5 Western meadowlark

Order Passeriformes, family Icteridae,
Sturnella neglecta

The western meadowlark nests on the
ground in drier grasslands of western
North America. Meadowlarks make a
typical nest by weaving grasses into
a round, cup-like shape. The cowbird
sometimes will lay its eggs in the
meadowlark's nest.

PLATE XXXVI

Red-eyed Vireo, Northern Oriole, Yellow Warbler,
Brown-headed Cowbird, and Scarlet Tanager

brown-headed cowbird yellow warbler cardinal

Scarlet Tanager (male)

Liz Vanderbilt

1 Red-eyed vireo

Order Passeriformes, family Vireonidae, *Vireo olivaceous*

The vireo's favorite foods are some of the nastiest and most destructive insects, making this species one of our best friends. This busy and adaptable creature can live in deciduous forests or in shade trees in residential areas. Weaving together fine strips of grapevine, bark, rootlet, vegetable fibers, and spider and caterpillar webs, the female shapes her nest into a cup. So varied are the materials she uses—paper, bits of hornet's nest, a medley of scraps—that it has been said that no two vireo nests are alike. Suspended, usually in a fork of twigs on the branch of a supple young tree, the nest sways in the wind.

2 Northern (Baltimore) oriole

Order Passeriformes, family Icteridae, *Icterus galbula*

The nest of the Baltimore oriole is a deep, gourd-shaped pocket that hangs by its rim (or strap) from thin branches or a fork high up in a tall tree. The female is the primary builder of the woven sack, which can be up to eight inches deep and has a three-inch opening at the top. She uses hair as well as bark and synthetic fibers, including grapevine, grasses, dogbane, milkweed, and Spanish moss. Orioles often return to the same territory but seldom reuse old nests. Their nests can be found when the trees are bare—like a calling card saying that orioles were here.

3 Yellow warbler, with a four-story nest

Order Passeriformes, family Parulidae, *Dendroica petechia*

A compact, cup-shaped dwelling, the yellow warbler nest is made of grass, weed stems, pieces of string, cotton wool, plant down, and other soft materials. It has an even softer lining of plant down, hair, and sometimes dandelion fluff. The female builds the nest, usually in low bushes like garden shrubs, but sometimes high in deciduous trees. While incubating the eggs, she is fed by her mate. Brown-headed cowbirds often invade this setting and lay their eggs in the warbler's nest, a situation dealt with effectively by the female yellow warbler. She builds a layer of nest material over the unwanted eggs so that they are kept from her insulating warmth. If the nest already contains her own eggs, the yellow warblers will usually hatch both kinds of eggs together, but sometimes they will begin again. The situation can result in a nest styled like an apartment building.

4 Brown-headed cowbird

Order Piciformes, family Icteridae, *Molothrus ater*

The insert below the cowbird compares a brown-headed cowbird egg (left) with a yellow warbler egg (center) and a cardinal egg (right). (See also plate XXXV.)

5 Scarlet tanager, male and female

Order Piciformes, family Thraupidae, *Piranga olivacea*

The female scarlet tanager builds her nest as a small cup of twigs, grass, and roots. The bright red male does his part by attracting predators elsewhere. He behaves like a ventriloquist, making his song sound like it is coming from a different place. He also eats insects that can become garden pests. The tanager nest is sometimes so loosely put together that you can see the eggs by looking up from below.

PLATE XXXVII

Robin, Vireos, Thrush, and Redstart

1 American robin, with nest

Order Passeriformes, family Turdidae, *Turdus migratorius*

Considered the herald of spring, the robin builds its nest in a dense shrub or tree or on a building ledge, from five to twenty feet off the ground. The female, sometimes assisted by the male, gathers twigs, grass, paper, and feathers. Inside the nest she spreads mud with her breast, then adds grass and other soft materials. An American robin can produce two to three broods in a year; on the average, however, only 40 percent successfully produce young. This robin is the largest North American member of the thrush family. Its name came from early English settlers, who likened its color to that of the British "robin redbreast," an unrelated European species, the Eurasian robin (*Erithacus rublicula*). Our robins are more closely related to English blackbirds (*Turdus merula*).

2 Solitary vireo

Order Passeriformes, family Vireonidae

(See plate XXXVI.)

3 Red-eyed vireo

Order Passeriformes, family Vireonidae, *Vireo olivaceous*

(See plate XXXVI.)

4 Swainson's thrush with nest

Order Passeriformes, family Turdidae, *Catharus ustulatus*

There are five different thrushes that fill our forests and sing their beautiful songs each spring and summer. Although they can nest near one another, they will not breed with each other because they only respond to their own distinctive song or call. The Swainson's thrush nest is only about 4 to 4.5 inches in diameter, but is a very sturdy cup of twigs, grass, mosses, and plant fibers. The female builds the nest in about four days.

5 American redstart (male and female)
Order Passeriformes, family Parulidae,
Setophaga ruticilla

American redstart with nest (male
above). This bird is sometimes called
the "little candle" or "little torch,"
bustling about protecting its territory
in eastern deciduous forests and collecting food. The nest is a cup of grass
and fibers, lined with grass, stems,
and hair in the fork of a tree or sapling.
It is sometimes bound with spider silk.
The female is the builder of this tiny
2.75-inch-diameter nest.

PLATE XXXVIII

Herons

ORDER CICONIIFORMES, FAMILY ARDEIDAE

1 Green-backed heron

Butorides virescens

The nest of the beautiful green-backed heron is a basket of sticks, placed in a small tree or shrub, usually near or over water, and in swampy thickets either in wetlands or near lowland forests. Nesting is often solitary, but can also be in small, loose colonies. The male green-backed heron chooses the nesting site before selecting a mate. He defends his territory before and after breeding, and mates with only one female per season. The male attracts the female using visual displays and the nesting site. Both the female and male make the nest: the male gathers the materials and the female constructs the nest.

2 Great blue heron

Ardea herodias

Great blue herons nest together throughout North America in colonies known as heronries or rookeries. In Oregon, heronries (from 15 to 160 nests) are found in a variety of tree species, including alder, cedar, hemlock, Douglas fir, spruce, cottonwood, and hawthorn. Most often, herons nest in alders over seventy-five feet tall; they can also nest on rocks, ledges, sea cliffs, and the ground. Long-legged herons might appear too awkward to nest in trees, but they are very good at weaving nests in high canopies. Their long toes grip branches and twigs and construct nests side by side. Each nest is a crude platform of sticks lined with finer twigs and grasses. The size of the heronry grows with the amount of food available nearby. In general, herons select nesting sites away from human activity. If disturbed during breeding season, the colony's reproductive rate can drop or adult herons will abandon the colony and move to a new site.

PLATE XXXIX

Tent Caterpillars ORDER LEPIDOPTERA

In what is known as an egg mass, some Lepidoptera adults lay from two hundred to five hundred eggs. After the eggs hatch, the adults leave the young. In some families the larvae scatter and try to survive on their own. In others the young stay together and live in a communal nest. This plate demonstrates three types of nest in which larvae grow together in host trees until they become adults and move on.

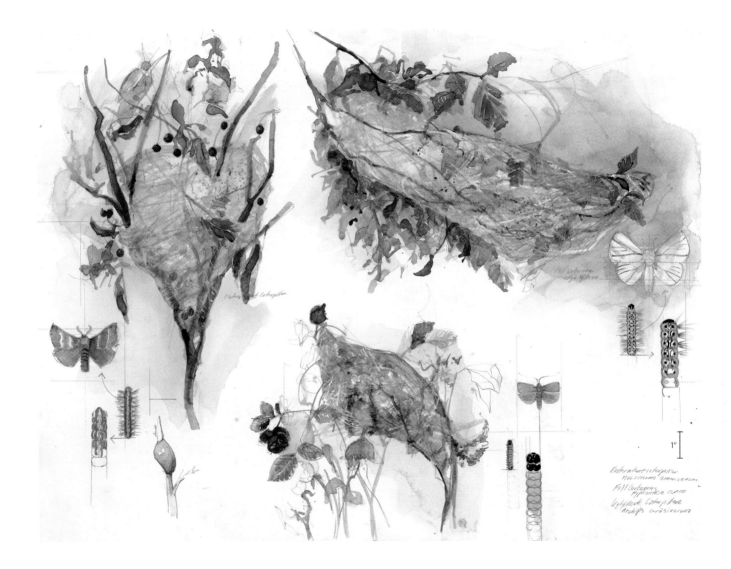

Eastern tent caterpillar

Malacosoma americanum

Fall webworm

Hyphantria cunea

Ugly nest Caterpillar

Archips cerasivorana

1"

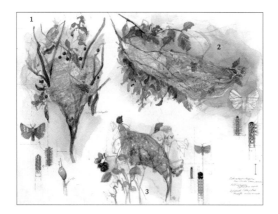

1 Eastern tent caterpillar

Order Lepidoptera, family Lasiocampidae, *Malacosoma americanum*

Eastern tent caterpillars build their silken nests at the base or "V" of two or more branches in the trunk area of such trees as cherry, plum, and peach (*Prunus*); apple and crabapple (*Malus*); hawthorns (*Crataegus*); and, sometimes, pear (*Pyrus*). They spin tent-like nests in which they live and venture forth to feed on leaves of their host tree. The tents grow as the caterpillars grow.

2 Fall webworm

Order Lepidoptera, family Arctiidae, *Hyphantria cunea*

The very tip of a branch is the location of choice for the fall webworm's nest. Some common host trees are birch (*Betula*), lilac (*Syrina*), crabapple (*Malus*), and cherry (*Prunus*). The insect can be damaging to the beauty of the tree, but is more of a nuisance than a threat to its health.

3 Uglynest caterpillar

Order Lepidoptera, family Tortricidae, *Archips cerasivorana*

This insect, found throughout the
northern states and Canada, builds
its nest in rose bushes or hawthorn or
cherry trees. Like the fall webworm,
it tends to destroy the tree's beauty
rather than its health. When the eggs
hatch in May or June, the larvae begin
building a web nest, where they remain until they emerge as moths. The
label "uglynest" probably refers to the
web around the feeding site becoming filled with their frass and bits of
leaves. In the mess they have created,
the larvae pupate.

PLATE XL

Bald-faced Hornets

ORDER HYMENOPTERA, FAMILY VESPIDAE, *Dolichovespula maculate*

A remarkable sequence of tasks in establishing the bald-faced hornet's nest can be credited to a single female, who was fertilized the previous year and survived the winter by hibernating in a sheltered spot. Unaided, she builds a small nest, lays eggs, collects food, and tends to her first brood, from which her future helpers emerge. She becomes queen of the new colony. She chooses a sheltered spot—a tree branch or roof beam—for the new nest. For building material she creates a kind of paper.

Using her mandibles, she shaves small particles of wood from beams, boards, or posts and adds saliva for cohesion. She uses the rapidly hardening paper pulp to make a stem, from which she suspends a very small comb. (The combs of hornets and wasps are horizontal and have hexagonal cells on the underside, each designed for one larva.) This central comb, which will house the brood, is then surrounded with a protective envelope of layers of paper, with only one flight hole left open at the bottom. The comb is soon extended into a multistoried building, with hornets adding story after story from the top downward, suspending each new comb from the one above by columnar supports. The hornets also extend the combs laterally. As the interior structure expands, the outer walls must be enlarged. Parts that are too close to the center are pulled down, and new ones, providing more space, are added. In this way, very large nests may develop in a single summer. Hornets can be observed building the outer walls of their nest. The color of the nests frequently appears gray because the hornets tend to collect their wood from the weathered surfaces of telephone poles, fence posts, or boards. But closer examination reveals a mosaic of colors depending on the source of the wood pulp.

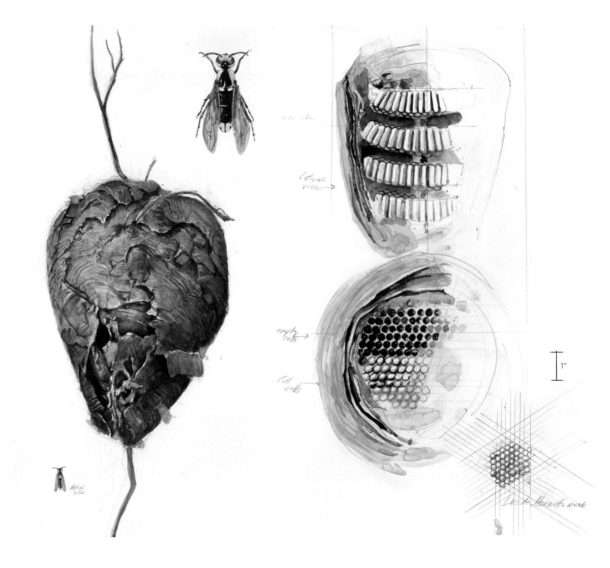

actual size

lateral view

empty cells

full cells

1"

PLATE XLI

Backyard Bees and Wasps
ORDER HYMENOPTERA

Entrance

1"

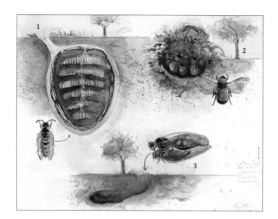

1 **Yellow jacket nest**

Family Vespidae, *Vespula* sp.

Yellow jackets create an elaborate underground nest built of paper. The form and material of the nest is similar to a bald-faced hornet's nest. The paper nest, created by mixing saliva and wood particles, can sometimes grow to the size of a basketball. A single queen begins the nest in the spring. When she has created enough workers to continue with the nest duties she remains inside and produces more insects. They begin by building a series of combs and then covering this comb with a layered envelope of paper. They often build these nests in ground cavities left by rodents and other mammals. They can also build above ground in trees and buildings.

2 **Bumblebee nest**

Family Apidae, *Bombus* sp.

In early spring queen bumblebees come out of hibernation and look for a place to start a colony. Common nesting sites include barns and abandoned animal holes in the ground. The queen is on her own to start the nest until her first brood of workers is able to help. Once the queen finds a spot she covers it with wax to protect it from moisture. The wax is produced in the abdominal skin glands and secreted in the form of small flakes. She mixes the wax with pollen to construct breeding cells. After a cell is filled with pollen, she lays a half dozen eggs in it and closes the cell with wax. After the eggs hatch, the larvae feed on the pollen; when mature they spin a cocoon to pupate. After four weeks the nest is completed and the first brood hatch as adults. The first brood is always the smallest due to lack of space and food in the new hive. They live for several weeks, and their tasks are to supply food, defend the nest, and build new breeding cells. Each new brood gets progressively larger until in summer the queens for the coming year and first males emerge from the cocoons. The nest cannot provide sufficient protection against low winter temperatures, nor will their food reserves take them through a whole winter. The colonies all die in late autumn, and only the fertilized queens who find shelter to make it through the winter survive.

3 Cicada killer wasp and nest

Family Sphecidae, *Sphecius speciosus*

In the summer there is quite a buzz-ing when a cicada killer wasp is flying with its prey to its nest in the ground, which is about six to ten inches deep and three inches wide. The cicada is paralyzed and will serve as prey for the wasp larvae. The wasp first deposits the cicada and then lays one egg and covers the nest with dirt. The male larva will need one cicada and the female will require two or three, because she will be twice as large as the male.

ARTIST'S NOTE: *Even for the most amateur entomologist, the cicada killer is easy to spot. First you hear it coming with its live prey, and then you see something about the size of a small hummingbird. You can follow them to their nests. The wasp is too occupied with its prey to notice you, so you are free to observe.*

ARTIST'S NOTE: *I was standing at the north entrance to the Field Museum waiting for an elevator to the third floor when I noticed an array of high-rise spiders and their webs extending up the glass windows facing the lake. Since most of the plates for this book were done from material in the museum's collections, it seems an appropriate subject for the final plate. The Field Museum's Dr. Petra Sierwald pointed out that "it's a species that's attracted to rocks overhanging water. . . . These high-rise buildings are just very big rocks overhanging water."*

PLATE XLII

High-rise Spider ORDER ARANEAE, FAMILY ARANEIDAE, *Larinioides sclopetarius*

Also called the bridge or gray cross spider, this spider is a large orb weaver that is often found on bridges and high buildings, especially around light and near water. They tend to live on steel objects and are not often seen on vegetation. What is most striking about this species' web is its durability. Their orb webs can have diameters of up to 70 centimeters (27.5 inches). Webs are often conspicuously close together, and frequently the web of a specimen is used to anchor the webs of one or more neighboring specimens. The females are larger than the males; females reach body lengths of about 1 centimeter (about .4 inches), males somewhat less. They often hide during the day, and wait for prey in the center of their web at night.

CONCLUSION

It's still dark out as I write this, but I'll be off for my walk in a minute. This cold winter morning I'll probably catch the sun coming up over the lake and see dozens of bird and insect nests that have already survived blustery winter storms. The exploration of what is close at hand has become second nature. I've been to the Amazon, Tanzania, and Madagascar, but my fascination for the natural world was born and is nurtured much closer to my home in Evanston, Illinois. During my childhood, my parents had a farm on the Wisconsin border. It was about three hundred acres, but it was the whole world. My mom wanted a lake, so my dad had an acre hole dug and she got the bonus of a "mountain." We paddled a canoe around this little pond, where there was wildlife in abundance. We sat in the barn (where my parents lived) and watched migrating sandhill cranes only a couple hundred yards away.

The illustrations in this book are designed to be our readers' own window on the natural world. The following bibliography we hope will tempt you to keep learning.

The word "ecology," taken from *oikos*, the Greek word for "home," means "study of home." That is what we have tried to offer here: a brief study of the homes of birds and insects. Thanks to the Field Museum and its scientists and educators for making this study possible by housing, exhibiting, and explaining the phenomenon of nests.

Conservation is born of affection. First you have to "meet" the world around you. And that means slowing down and looking. Once you do, your curiosity will compel you to keep looking. Prompted by the elegant solutions that you see all around you, you may just be inspired enough to want to protect what's out there. Our brief study concluded with a few local nests. I've always wondered where bumble bees kept their nests. . . . I never realized so much was going on under my feet. I hope this book sets you off on a similarly rich journey, close to home.

PEGGY MACNAMARA

ACKNOWLEDGMENTS

I would like to thank Nancy Deneen, who laboriously edited the entire manuscript and made numerous text improvements, and Laura Nelson, who researched and edited parts of the text.

And most important, I would like to thank the scientists of the zoology department of the Field Museum, who offered invaluable advice and assistance.

FURTHER READING

Borror, D. J., C. A. Triplehorn, and N. F. Johnson. 1989. *An Introduction to the Study of Insects.* 6th ed. New York: Saunders College Publishing.

Collias, N. E., and E. C. Collias. 1976. *External Construction by Animals.* Stroudsburg, PA: Dowden, Hutchinson and Ross.

Forsyth, A. 1989. *The Architecture of Animals.* Richmond Hill, ON: Camden House.

Hadlington, P. 1996. *Australian Termites and Other Common Timber Pests.* Sydney, NSW: UNSW Press.

Hansell, M. H. 1984. *Animal Architecture and Building Behavior.* New York: Longman.

Hegh, E. 1922. *Les Termites.* Brussels: Louis Desmet-Verteneuil.

Jolivet, P., and K. K. Verma. 2005. *Fascinating Insects: Some Aspects of Insect Life.* Philadelphia: Pensoft Publishers.

Skaife, S. H. 1955. *Dwellers in Darkness: An Introduction to the Study of Termites.* New York: Longmans Green.

von Frisch, K. 1974. *Animal Architecture.* New York: Harcourt Brace Jovanovich.

Wilson, E. O. 1971. *Insect Societies.* Cambridge, MA: Harvard University Press.

———. 1990. *The Ants*. Cambridge, MA: Belknap Press. Winner of the Pulitzer Prize, with Bert Hölldobler.
———. 1994. *Journey to the Ants: A Story of Scientific Exploration*. Cambridge, MA: Belknap Press. With
  Bert Hölldobler.
Wood, J. G. 1866. *Homes Without Hands*. New York: Harper and Brothers.

WEB SITES
The Cornell lab or ornithology: www.birds.cornell.edu/AllAboutBirds/.
For species names: http://en.wikipedia.org/wiki/Bird.